LOOKING FORWARD
to the REST
of YOUR LIFE?

LOOKING FORWARD
to the REST
of YOUR LIFE?

Embracing Midlife and Beyond

LORRY LUTZ

Baker Books
A Division of Baker Book House Co
Grand Rapids, Michigan 49516

Published by Baker Books
a division of Baker Book House Company
P.O. Box 6287, Grand Rapids, MI 49516-6287
www.bakerbooks.com

Printed in the United States of America

Library of Congress Cataloging-in-Publication Data

Lutz, Lorry.
    Looking forward to the rest of your life? : embracing midlife and beyond / Lorry Lutz.
        p.   cm.
    Includes bibliographical references.
    ISBN 0-8010-6459-7 (pbk.)
    1. Middle aged women—Religious life. 2. Aged women—Religious life. 3. Christian women—Religious life. 4. Aging—Religious aspects—Christianity. I. Title.
    BV4579.5.L87 2004
    248.8′43—dc22   2003026901

Unless otherwise indicated, Scripture quotations are taken from the HOLY BIBLE, NEW INTERNATIONAL VERSION®. NIV®. Copyright © 1973, 1978, 1984 by International Bible Society. Used by permission of Zondervan. All rights reserved.

Scripture marked GNT is taken from the Good News Translation—Second Edition Copyright © 1992 by American Bible Society. Used by permission.

Scripture marked MESSAGE is taken from THE MESSAGE. Copyright © by Eugene H. Peterson 1993, 1994, 1995. Used by permission of NavPress Publishing Group.

Scripture marked TLB is taken from *The Living Bible* © 1971. Used by permission of Tyndale House Publishers, Inc., Wheaton, IL 60189. All rights reserved.

Scripture marked NIVI is taken from the HOLY BIBLE, NEW INTERNATIONAL VER-SION, Copyright © 1973, 1978, 1984 by International Bible Society. First published in Great Britain 1979. Inclusive Language Version 1995, 1996. Used by permission of Hodder & Stoughton, a member of the Hodder Headline Group. ALL RIGHTS RESERVED.

Scripture marked RSV is taken from the Revised Standard Version of the Bible, copyright 1946, 1952, 1971 by the Division of Christian Education of the National Council of the Churches of Christ in the USA. Used by permission.

To my granddaughters

Tamarah
Andrea
Bronwyn
Johannah
Hollie
Bonnie Rachel
Dilarah
Joellah
Rachelle
Deborah
Sarah
Suzannah

May they keep their eyes on the finish line

CONTENTS

To finish well I will intentionally and joyfully in every circumstance pursue the purpose for which God uniquely created me to the very end, trusting in every circumstance that he is always with me, faithful, loving, and strong.

"God is not unjust; he will not forget your work and the love you have shown him as you have helped his people and continue to help them. We want each of you to show this same diligence *to the very end*."

Hebrews 6:10–11, emphasis mine

ACKNOWLEDGMENTS

This project would never have happened without the hundreds of women I've met who are living their lives to the fullest to the very end. A special word of thanks to the ten women who serve as models of "finishing well" and for their willingness to reveal the intimate details of their lives. Eliza and Blanche already are enjoying their eternal rewards.

I'm deeply grateful to Emily Voorhies and Global Action for helping with the development and analysis of the Fifty Plus Questionnaire. I'm also grateful to the more than 250 women who responded, giving me insights and perspective on what aging means to them. Thanks to the focus groups in Colorado Springs, Milwaukee, Minneapolis, and Birmingham who so candidly expressed the joys and difficulties of growing older.

I appreciate the time pastors gave me to share their insights about working with senior adults—JoAnn Brechbill, John Bristol, Dallas Shafer, Ken Kilinski, Rosalyn Staples, Nancy Schell, Jim Poyner, and Carl Vogelaar.

I'm grateful to Ethel Herr and her critique group in California who gave their time to read and help me improve the manuscript. What a labor of love. Thanks to Jan Kyne for her usual creative suggestions.

As every writer knows, a book without a publisher is like a pregnancy without a birth. This is the second time I've had the privilege of working with the qualified and motivated staff at Baker Book House. Bob Hosack, acquisitions editor, took the risk to accept my earlier work, *Women as Risk-Takers for God,* and encouraged me from the very beginning to pursue my dreams about this new book. Mary Wenger gave her gentle and professional guidance to bring the manuscript to its final stages. Many others were involved, but I want to give a special thanks to Diane Whisner, who designed the attractive cover, which says it all.

And an overwhelming sense of gratitude to my husband, Al, who read every word as it came off the printer; he was my most serious critic. How many times I heard his cheerful "Lunch is ready" as I was struggling to put a sentence together just right. His greatest encouragement came when he returned the last chapter with tears in his eyes.

HOW I LEARNED I WAS A "LITTLE OLD LADY"

Not at fifty or even sixty did I consider myself old—certainly not when the first Denny's waitress offered me a senior discount. Becoming a grandmother at age fifty-one had added excitement to my life but also an empty longing, for my grandson lived more than seven hundred miles away. Over the years I could proudly report the arrival of one grandchild after another, until there were eighteen. As grandparents, my husband and I loved them, showered them with gifts, and displayed their pictures to anyone who would look. We even traveled halfway around the globe to visit them.

My sixty-second birthday brought an exciting new venture of quite another sort, for that year I started traveling globally as the director of the AD2000 & Beyond Women's Track. For the next ten years I taught Christian women leaders around the world and met godly women who showed me what living for Christ could mean in the toughest of circumstances.

When seventy arrived my children tempered the shock by planning a joyous birthday celebration. I felt rich as children and grandchildren crowded around me and helped me blow out the candles.

Of course I didn't think I "looked" seventy! Kind friends and international women massaged my ego by saying, "You don't *look* that old." Refusing to look old, I worked on keeping up a youthful appearance. I colored my hair, avoided "Grandma styles" like cardigan sweaters and polyester dresses, and tried to keep up with fashions. I succumbed to all the cultural pressures to look younger than my age!

I prided myself that many of my friends were younger than I—probably because I worked with active women who were leaders in their own right. I read broadly and followed the news avidly to avoid becoming the out-of-date stereotype and because I needed to be knowledgeable about missions and global issues.

All my efforts notwithstanding, clear signs emerged that I was becoming a senior. Social security checks and IRA distributions began arriving. Retiring from full-time ministry brought freedom to do the things I felt God wanted me to do without going regularly to an office or dealing with all the responsibilities that leading a ministry brings. Surprisingly the change felt good.

Aging wasn't so bad after all; in fact my husband of more than fifty years and I found it to be an enriching and meaningful stage of life. But I remember the day I knew I was old and that others thought so too.

A Christian organization had considered me for a board position. I looked forward to contributing from my years of experience in ministry without having the responsibility of implementing the ideas and programs. And then to my shock I was told, "We can't have you on the board. We have a rule that board members cannot be over seventy years old."

Suddenly I felt valueless. Did they see me as someone who would hold back the forward movement of the organization? Were my ideas no longer worth considering? I felt like a "little old lady."

God used this experience to remind me that my value does not lie in what I know or what I do, but who I am because of his grace. What other people think of me is not really important as long as my passion to serve him drives me obediently to his Word and listening for his direction. I matter to him at every stage of life. He considers me valuable. His faithfulness over the years has proven that beyond a doubt.

This experience also brought into sharp focus that many women face this sense of worthlessness as they grow older. God has given me a passion to encourage and mobilize women to serve him, and I saw the clear mandate to write a book that would help women like you prepare to face the new challenges of the years ahead. So many women have told me that, now that their children are grown, they have time on their hands, but they don't know what to do with it.

Now well into my seventies, I am thankful that God has continued to show me more ways to serve him. I pray that in the pages to follow you will feel encouraged to begin at whatever stage you find yourself to prepare for your "bonus years." I also pray that you won't consider yourself without purpose because your nest is empty or think that you are a burden to others.

Over the years I've met many women of God who have demonstrated what it means to "finish well." It's been my privilege to learn the secrets of their success. I'm pleased to be able to share the stories of some of these models, who represent just a few examples of the many different ways God gifts and uses us. As you read them I pray you will find applications to help you look forward to finishing your journey well.

Women are living longer than ever before. You may likely do the same. After reaching the empty nest stage many may still have another forty years of life ahead. What are you going to do with that second half of life?

The following dialogue from a Jewish tale poignantly describes our dilemma.

> A young woman once said to an old woman,
> "What is life's heaviest burden?"
> And the old woman said, "To have nothing to carry."[1]

To finish well we must carry in our hearts the compassionate love of Christ and in our hands the gifts he has given us to share that love with others.

Vonette Bright

A REVERED ELDER STATESWOMAN

In 1951 Bill and Vonette Bright cofounded Campus Crusade for Christ, a worldwide ministry of evangelism and discipleship. By the end of the 1990s Campus Crusade was active in 186 countries. Though Bill and Vonette partnered closely together, Vonette gradually realized the need to develop and use her own gifts. The Brights demonstrate a unique balance of partnership in ministry as well as using their individual gifts to accomplish God's purpose for them. I interviewed Vonette sixteen months before Bill died in July 2003.

"I'm spending more time in doctors' offices these days. And I spend more time exercising. I stretch fifteen to twenty minutes before I even get out of bed in the morning," says Vonette Bright.

At seventy-five, Vonette is candid about her life as a senior adult. Always beautifully groomed, her blond hair softly framing her delicately lined face, Vonette looks the picture of health. But while she admits to arthritis and other unnamed issues, she is positive and upbeat about the direction of her life now.

"There's a lot of relaxedness in my life right now. I can't do the frivolous things. People expect greater wisdom now, and I think I have some answers that I didn't have when I was younger."

Bill's terminal illness constantly reminded them both of the shortness of time, and Vonette faced practical issues as well.

"I am adjusting to convenience, putting things lower on the shelves. I'm learning that material things don't matter. Where would I put anything more? I'm giving some things away."

Yet age, health issues, and her husband's illness did not dampen Vonette's desire to serve God in whatever way she could. At seventy-one she launched a weekly radio spot called *Women Today*, which is heard on Christian radio stations all over the country.

"I have two books in the making," Vonette explains. "One is about the practicalness of the Spirit-filled life. And I'm trying a novel for the first time."

The novel idea emerged after Bill's first novel with Ted Dekker, *Blessed Child*, became a success. Bill urged Vonette to try her hand at fiction, believing that stories can sometimes get a message across better than straight teaching. Vonette enlisted an experienced novelist to help her fashion the story, while she developed the theology and problem resolution the women in her book face, and thus *The Sister Circle* was birthed.

Of course, Vonette's major task was to take care of Bill Bright in his struggle with pulmonary fibrosis. Theirs was a partnership that went back more than fifty years to when they grew up in the same Oklahoma town. Bill's parents were influential ranchers in Cowleta, a town of fifteen hundred that had been settled by a number of sophisticated families.

The Brights' home was the center of rural entertainment for the town's youth—hayrides, ice-cream socials, watermelon feasts. Vonette remembers listening to Bill's winning national oration when he was a senior. Though she was only a seventh-grader the thought passed through her mind, "He's going to be a great man. That's the kind of man I'd love to marry one day."

But Vonette had no romantic thoughts about Bill Bright then; she was too busy pursuing her own teenage dreams. Her mother encouraged Vonette and her brother in every way possible to excel at school. She saw to it that they had dance lessons and trained them to perform at church functions. If Vonette had a recitation to give at a church program, her mother would take her to the church the day before and stand in the back calling out to Vonette, "Louder—I can't hear you."

To this day Vonette credits her mother for her own independent and ambitious spirit. "I had great inspiration from my mother. She was an activist. She pushed us [my brother and me] to the front."

Vonette's mother took a serious role in her husband's business. She went to work in his filling station, pumping gas and keeping the books. Later, during the Second World War, she worked as acting postmistress, hiring country girls to work at her home while she was away.

Vonette muses, "I used to think Bill became interested in me because he liked Mother so much and that I would be like her. Bill believed that women have real discernment and are some of the best managers. He felt that any business needed a woman's insight."

Just after completing her first year at Texas Women's University, Vonette received a letter out of the blue from Bill, who was now running his own business in California—the Bright California Confections. Bill wrote that he had seen a young movie actress who, he said, reminded him of Vonette. She didn't even bother to answer his brief note for several months. After all, they had barely seen or spoken to each other since he left for college. But that began a whirlwind romance by mail.

"Before you knew it," Vonette remembers, "we were writing every day. I was receiving candy and flowers. As a businessman he was able to pay for all the expenses that most college guys couldn't do.

"He came in March and took me to the big ball on campus. He gave me the biggest orchid I'd ever seen and proposed to me on that first night. As a new Christian he felt God told him, 'Vonette is to be your wife.'"

Listening to Vonette's story one cannot help but recognize the providential direction of God upon the lives of these two people. The design for Campus Crusade for Christ, the worldwide impact of the ministry of this man and woman, and the miraculous provisions all rested on their response to God's plan for them.

Strange as it may seem, Vonette was not a true believer at this time. She thought she was a Christian; she attended church and lived a moral life. But when Bill began writing her about the things God was teaching him, asking her questions about Scripture he was reading and giving her prayer requests, Vonette was uncomfortable with his ideas.

At her parents' insistence, Vonette and Bill had agreed not to marry until she completed college. Even then, they wanted her to take a teaching job locally first. After graduation Vonette determined to visit Bill in California—to salvage the relationship and hopefully straighten him out about his religious zeal.

"I was going to tell him that it's okay to be a Christian, but you don't have to be one-sided about this. I thought Bill was going to give up these fanatical ideas or I would be coming home without a ring."

In California Bill introduced her to many of his friends who impressed Vonette. "They knew where they were going; they talked about God so freely. I didn't know faith could be so exciting."

Bill recognized her lack of faith, and Vonette saw that she could not change him. "I didn't want to stand in his way. It was so right for him, but I couldn't go along with it," she explains.

Convinced that God had selected Vonette to be his wife, Bill introduced her to his Sunday school teacher and mentor, Dr. Henrietta Mears. As Dr. Mears explained the plan of salvation, everything began to fall into place for Vonette. After three days she realized that God had a purpose for her life and that she was foolish not to trust him.

Bill and Vonette were married in Cowleta in December of 1948. On their honeymoon Bill set the pattern of their many years together when he told Vonette, "I'm marrying you as my partner. I want you to make it your business to investigate the things I'm involved in. I want to be able to discuss things with you. I don't want you to become just Mrs. William Bright. I want you to be your own person."

Though their first few years of married life seemed relatively normal, Vonette had no idea what that commitment would mean. She taught school while Bill ran three businesses—the Bright California Confections; an oil business with interests in oil fields and drilling equipment; and a purchasing service. Bill also was attending the newly founded Fuller Theological Seminary part-time. On weekends he joined a team of young people from Hollywood Presbyterian Church with the encouragement of Dr. Mears to visit college campuses to share their faith. Along with Louis Evans Jr. and Gary Demarest they mobilized teams to go to the fraternities and organized girls to go to the sororities. Vonette didn't have the joy or confidence in personal evangelism that her husband had, but she also joined a team.

One morning after a long night of study for a Greek exam, Bill came home ecstatic. During the night God had shown him what he wanted him to do. He would help reach the entire world for Jesus Christ by starting out with college students.

Vonette listened awestruck as her husband talked a mile a minute. They'd sell their businesses and move to the campus. They'd live by faith. Just the night before as they had talked and prayed together over their future, they had signed a "contract" to be slaves of Jesus. And Bill was sure this was what God meant by that commitment.

But Vonette didn't know anything about living by faith. "I was scared to death. I could see myself in a little cotton dress buttoned down the front and tennis shoes. We both had very materialistic ideas. I didn't want to dampen his spirits, but I was hardly able to concentrate on what he was saying."

Vonette's mind was in a whirl. She tried to persuade Bill to hang on to some of his businesses. When he talked about giving one away Vonette retorted, "Not on your life!"

True to his honeymoon promise of partnership, Bill asked her to come up with a plan; what would it cost to live for a year? She figured they would need $2400 above the $2400 she was earning as a teacher.

A few days later Bill came home to tell her that the man who had been running Bright's Purchasing Service offered to buy the business for $2400. Bill chided her, "Can't you see this is of God?"

When he was offered a very generous consulting fee for one day a month, Vonette urged him, "Bill, take it; take it." But Bill refused, believing the devil would use this to keep their eyes on material things. Living by faith meant exactly that.

One day after school Vonette knelt at her bed and confessed her fears to God. "I don't know anything that Bill wants to do. I'm just scared to death. You've got to give me the heart to respond."

In response God gave Vonette a heart and vision attuned with Bill's as together they cofounded Campus Crusade for Christ. God even gave her joy in personal evangelism. The first year after she was able to quit her teaching job, she began stepping out in faith, meeting girls on the UCLA campus where they now lived. "The first fifty women with whom I made appointments all received Christ," she recalls. She remembers the excitement of saying to Bill, "I know now what Dr. Mears meant when she [once told me], 'Find your place marked X.'"

Over the next twenty years Vonette poured her life into Bill's interests. As his partner, she sat on boards and planning committees, traveled with him as he shared the challenge of reaching students for Christ, and served as a sounding board for his ideas and dreams.

Sometimes Vonette must have felt like an army wife, moving from cottage to campus; leaving her own home to sharing a home with Dr. Mears; and relocating to Arrowhead Springs in San Bernardino, which became the headquarters of Campus Crusade.

Bill continued to encourage her involvement in the ministry even after their sons were born. Vonette recalls, "When the children were little he would come home from the office to stay with them so that I could go and speak someplace, in

order to make it possible for me to have a personal ministry."
She spent many hours writing training curriculum after the
children were in bed, adjusting her schedule to meet their
needs. She was also grateful for the Campus Crusade "family"
living on the headquarters site, who often shared child-care
so busy mothers could be involved in ministry.

By the end of the sixties Campus Crusade for Christ was active in twenty-five countries; the Four Spiritual Laws had been
written and translated into many languages; and plans were
being made for EXPLO 72, where they expected 85,000 students
to converge on the Dallas Cotton Bowl. During this time God
brought four young men from the Harvard Business School to
help Bill. (One of the four, Steve Douglas, is president of Campus
Crusade today.) Not only were they in love with Jesus but they
also had their fingers on the pulse of America's youth culture
and longed to share with others what he'd done for them.

Vonette was thrilled with what she saw God doing through
Bill's dream and with the commitment of faith they'd made.
But she felt a quiet discontent in her heart. "Suddenly no one
was asking me questions. I wasn't being consulted on big issues, on directions. I felt lost."

Vonette began seeking if God had something just for her,
something that would use her gifts to glorify him and at the
same time fit into Bill's vision and plans. On December 6, 1971,
Vonette read in her devotions about Peter and John being released from prison (Acts 4:23–32). God revealed to her that
the believers were united together in prayer in the midst of a
decadent, rebellious people.

"What would happen if we could unite the women of this
nation to pray?" she thought. She'd already talked with leading
Christian women such as Ruth Graham and Millie Dienert, Billy
Graham's "first lady of prayer," about the need for Christian
women to unite so they could make a stronger impact in the
world. That night the vision became crystal clear, and the
concept of the Great Commission Prayer Crusade was born.
It became the prayer support for a number of major national
and international events, uniting people to pray and getting

churches to cooperate across interdenominational lines. All this happened out of Vonette's office with the blessing of her husband. The Great Commission Prayer Crusade eventually became the prayer arm of Campus Crusade for Christ.

Even as Vonette spoke and wrote and interacted with her husband and staff, her influence broadened beyond Campus Crusade. In 1976 she became a member of the Lausanne Committee for World Evangelization—one of three women and forty-seven men. Vonette did not feel intimidated as a "token woman." "I've been used to this; I've been sitting on committees [with men]. I have a husband who made me a partner the minute we were married. I had the opportunity to exert some influence.

"Women are very important to meetings like this because they offer a woman's perspective. Many times men aren't thinking of women or of families. They'd talk about strategies and I'd say, 'Men, think of women; here are opportunities to put women to work. They're available if you would ask them.'"

By 1977, at the age of fifty, Vonette wrote her first book, *For Such a Time as This.* She has since written twelve books, including her novel. She continued to work with cooperative prayer groups and in 1983, at age fifty-six, became the chairperson of the National Day of Prayer. Five years later the National Prayer Committee successfully lobbied to get a bill through Congress making the first Thursday of every May a national day of prayer. It passed unanimously!

Campus Crusade moved its headquarters to Orlando, Florida, in 1992. Vonette felt this was a new beginning for her. She turned the National Day of Prayer over to Shirley Dobson, wife of James Dobson of Focus on the Family, the Great Commission Prayer Crusade to Ben Jennings, and resigned from the Lausanne Committee.

At sixty-five Vonette was not retiring—simply refining. She redefined her spiritual gifts. "I think gifts change from time to time. I've had the gift of administration, the gift of discernment, the gift of hospitality. I think God gives us gifts for whatever he's called us to do."

Her boundless energy may have been abating, but her passion for evangelism and discipleship never waned. She recognizes that as a multi-gifted person, she has the responsibility to be a good steward of the talents God has given her.

An old friend of the Brights', Dr. Henry Brandt, used to say, "There are one-ring circuses, two-ring circuses, five-ring circuses. Find out what kind of circus you can run. If you can run a five-ring, and you can keep all these balls bouncing at the same time and keep your emotional equilibrium working, then go for the five-ring."

Vonette found this comforting when she was balancing children, husband, and ministry. Even with more physical limitations, she was eager to keep every ring going that she could.

In later years she focused on writing, sharing from her rich experience of many years in the ministry. Her weekly radio spot grew out of these experiences and the contacts she has had with thousands of people, rich and poor, famous and ordinary, around the world.

Though they had not lost their vision, in 2000 she and Bill began talking about passing on the torch of leadership. In a fiftieth-anniversary report of the history of Campus Crusade, Bill wrote, "As I come to the beginning of the new millennium, and the fiftieth year of Campus Crusade, my vision and urgency for helping fulfill the Great Commission is greater than ever. . . . My zeal . . . continues unabated."

Before they were ready to announce Bill's replacement, the blow that changed their lives struck. After struggling with a chronic cough for many months Bill went to Mayo Clinic, where he was told he had pulmonary fibrosis, a terminal lung disease. He was placed on twenty-four-hour oxygen and told he had a year to live.

"When we heard the news at Mayo we went back to our room," Vonette recalls. "I said, 'Honey, look at this. We've had fifty-one years of marriage and fifty years of ministry. We know your successor. What person is able to say that?' We began to count our blessings—the children are grown; the ministry is on its feet.

"I've had some tears; what am I going to do? One of the wonderful things that has happened is that God has shown me there's life after Bill Bright. I trust I'll be able to handle [being alone]. As long as I live I want to be productive. I know that if God keeps me alive he has something for me to do. I'm expecting to have that revelation from him when he takes Bill."

Bill and Vonette found the days of uncertain waiting precious. There was a tremendous peace and joy. With alternative medical treatment Bill grew stronger, able to work from his home, and even took speaking engagements. His passion was to put in writing everything that God has for him to say, and he had ideas for ten books lined up.

At first Vonette wouldn't leave Bill's side, but she found that he could do more things for himself than she thought. One morning he called her at her office to say that he'd cleaned up the kitchen and turned the dishwasher on.

"Bill and I thanked God for what we were learning. This was a new adventure. We'd never faced this before. We had some of the sweetest times we've ever had in our lives. Such a sweet relationship, just dear. I can't complain."

On July 19, 2003 Bill Bright entered the presence of his Lord. "Vonette described his passing as peaceful. She said as the time drew near she told him, 'Honey, I want you to go and be with Jesus, and I know that's what you want and what Jesus wants. So why don't you just crawl up into his arms and let him carry you away?' She says she turned away for a moment, looked back, and 'he was gone.'"[2]

Vonette clings to the promises God gives her:

> I will lead the blind by ways they have not known,
>   along unfamiliar paths I will guide them;
> I will turn the darkness into light before them
>   and make the rough places smooth.
> These are the things I will do;
> I will not forsake them.
>
>   Isaiah 42:16

ONE

BIBLICAL MODELS:

Facing the Future with Vision and Grace

Even though on the outside it often looks as though things are falling apart on us, on the inside, where God is making new life, not a day goes by without his unfolding grace.

2 Corinthians 4:16 (MESSAGE)

As character directs aging, aging reveals character.

James Hillman, *The Force of Character*

Most of us are in denial about growing old. At forty or fifty life is so full of responsibilities and fulfilling relationships that we find it easy to ignore the passing years. But when we reach sixty or seventy, even though we don't feel old, our birthdays tell us we are! High school or college years seem but yesterday, and before we know it, retirement looms before us.

All too soon we reach the psalmist's outer limits, which prompted him to write, "The length of our days is seventy years—or eighty, if we have the strength; yet their span is but trouble and sorrow, for they quickly pass, and we fly away" (Ps. 90:10).

Why does God allow our bodies—these complex and matchless creations—to deteriorate? (Of course we know the answer—that debacle in the garden!) We see the hunched backs, the shuffling gaits, the thinning hair, and we deny that we will ever look like that. But we very likely will! Can we prepare for this time of life so it has value, meaning, and joy?

What does the Bible say about aging—to us as we age and as we watch others age? Scripture does not provide a systematic theology of aging, or detailed instructions about how to face growing old, or what to do when we get there. But precious promises encourage us that good things lie ahead when we walk with God. David experienced this as he reveled in God's promise: "Even to your old age and gray hairs I am he, I am he who will sustain you. I have made you and I will carry you; I will sustain you and I will rescue you" (Isa. 46:4).

As we pass through the disappointments, the losses, and the difficult decisions of life, we gain experience and hopefully wisdom. To his accusers Job declared, "Is not wisdom found among the aged? Does not long life bring understanding?" (Job 12:12).

In his suffering and confusion Job must have thought a lot about life's end. Even in his darkest hours he was comforted to know: "The days of mortals are determined. You [God] have decreed the number of their months and have set limits they cannot exceed" (Job 14:5 NIV). So whether God decrees a long life with its possible loneliness, illness, or dementia, or on the other hand, its vigor, strength, and creativity, we should be prepared to live life to his fullest purpose for us.

The Bible gives us models of women who found God's purpose for them through a long life. They lived in a patriarchal society where women were deemed possessions with roles defined basically as prolific producers of children (primarily sons) and sources of labor; they were viewed as a valuable asset but with few rights or even opportunities for self-development. Yet consider the character and strength of some of these women through their long lives.

Sarah — Fruitful in Old Age (Genesis 16–22)

Known for her physical beauty, Sarah emerges as the first elderly woman we read of in the Bible. She lived with her husband, Abraham, until she was 127 years old, most of that time unfulfilled and barren.

Both Abraham and Sarah longed to have a child and grieved over her empty womb. God had promised, "A son coming from your own body will be your heir" (Gen. 15:4). They must have wondered many times if they had misheard his voice. Miraculously for both of them, at ninety years of age, Sarah became pregnant and delivered a son, Isaac.

Only God's intervention could bring about Sarah's miraculous pregnancy, but we can apply her fruitfulness in old age as a model in other ways.

Sarah's life was difficult enough—getting along with her servant Hagar, who bore Abraham a son, Ishmael, and treating Ishmael fairly must have been trying. No doubt strained relationships developed with their nephew Lot and his family, which eventually resulted in the two families separating over property disputes. None of these stressed her like God's call upon Abraham to sacrifice Isaac. We'll never know how Sarah reacted and if she had the faith to believe, as Abraham did, that God would provide the ram for the burnt offering.

Jewish Talmudic resources say Sarah refused to live with Abraham from this point on because of shock and grief, which eventually caused her death.

As the years go by, life becomes more difficult for all of us, both physically and emotionally. We will face pain and suffering, death of loved ones, disappointments, and loneliness. God will ask us to trust him even when he seems to be asking the impossible. But he wants us, like Sarah, to continue to fulfill his purpose for us to the very end.

God longs that his children produce fruit as long as he gives them life. The psalmist promises, "The righteous will flourish like a palm tree, they will grow like a cedar of Lebanon; . . . They will still bear fruit in old age, they will stay fresh and green" (Ps. 92:12, 14). This is his desire and should be ours.

Deborah — A Woman of Influence for Many Years (Judges 4–5)

Deborah grew up during a time of political uncertainty and enemy oppression. The Canaanites, who had ruled over Israel for twenty years, controlled the economy and the roads, extorting money from travelers and killing any who resisted.

Deborah must have had a softhearted dad, for he named her "honey-bee." Perhaps like most Jewish girls of that time, she married young, and she and her husband Lappidoth settled in Bethel in the relatively safe hills north of Judea, where no doubt they began raising their family. Deborah would later refer to herself as a "mother in Israel," which meant either her motherhood or her position in the land.

Over the years the Israelites began to recognize that Deborah had great wisdom and the ability to resolve conflicts. In spite of the dangers on the road of Canaanite ambush, people came from every part of the country, sneaking along the rugged trails to avoid the main roads where the militant occupiers waited to attack, to ask Deborah for her advice and counsel. Deborah set up her "office" under the Palm of Deborah, acting as counselor, prophetess, and judge—virtually the prime minister. God had chosen her, a woman, as Israel's deliverer. She did not arrive at this high place of leadership by accident, or because God could not find a suitable man, but because he wanted to use her and the extraordinary gifts he had given her.

God spoke directly to Deborah, instructing her to call Barak—a general without troops or weapons—to recruit an army and attack the Canaanites. Barak must have thought the idea ridiculous. How could he defeat the Canaanites? They had more than nine hundred chariots and hundreds of spears, while the Israelites were unarmed and unorganized.

Barak was smart enough to recognize that Deborah was a prophetess of God, a leader endowed with wisdom and spiritual insight. He insisted that she accompany him to the northern part of the country to help recruit ten thousand men and guide him in the difficult decisions he would have to make.

Deborah left her home (and presumably her family) and traveled sixty miles north with Barak. When the army was recruited, she instructed Barak when and how to attack, confident in God's promise that they would win the battle. In turn, God sent a flood that swept Sisera's chariots away, routing the enemy.

God graciously responded to the repentant cry of the Israelites who finally came to their senses. He rescued them from their oppressors—as he would do thirteen times in the Book of Judges. Each time they repented he raised up a judge to deliver them. As long as the judge ruled, the Israelites obeyed God's commands and the land was peaceful.

During Deborah's incumbency, the land had peace for forty years (Judges 5:31). She continued to serve God and his people well into old age—a challenge we should not ignore.

Naomi — God's Faithfulness in Old Age (Ruth 1–4)

Naomi experienced great sorrow and disappointment throughout her life only to find God's extraordinary blessing and comfort in her later years.

Naomi's husband, Elimelech, had moved his wife and two sons across the border to Moab to escape the famine devastating Judea. It was not easy to leave family and friends, home and comfort to go to a foreign country. Naomi had to learn to accommodate herself to the strange customs of the Moabites and accept their angry looks and derogatory comments about these "Jewish intruders." Though she clung to the love of

Yahweh, she was surrounded by pagans who worshipped Chemosh, the Moabite god.

After a few years in Moab Elimelech died. By now Naomi's sons were old enough for marriage. She would have preferred that they go home and choose Jewish girls, but the boys married Moabite women, so she stayed on to be near them. She was comforted, however, that her daughters-in-law, Orpah and Ruth, loved and accepted her. Before they could bear children however, both their husbands died. Naomi was now a widow, childless and with no hope of grandchildren, living in a foreign land without any source of income.

One would expect to read of a depressed, hopeless woman shrinking into her home, alienated from her neighbors, nursing her grief in anger against God. But Naomi had not lost her faith in God nor her spirit of independence. Instead, hearing that the Judean famine was over, she announced to her daughters-in-law that she was returning home. She urged them to find some nice Moabite boys, marry, and have children, since she could not bear more sons to become their husbands.

In the end Naomi's daughter-in-law Ruth insisted on returning with her to Judea in a beautiful story of "in-law love." Once back in Bethlehem with her old friends Naomi seemed to crash briefly, succumbing to self-pity. "Don't call me Naomi," she declared. "Call me Mara, because the Almighty has made my life very bitter" (Ruth 1:20).

But God had planned a sweet ending. In his providential care Ruth met Boaz, her kinsman-redeemer, who under Jewish law took responsibility to marry the widow and continue the bloodline. Their marriage produced for Naomi a precious grandson, Obed, a direct ancestor of King David and ultimately Jesus. Her spirits lifted, Naomi became the doting grandmother; her friends rejoiced with her in a daughter-in-law who loved her more than seven sons and a son-in-law who provided for her in her old age.

Many women like Naomi have been battered by life, facing disappointment and hurt. Solutions seem impossible; the future looks hopeless. But they make decisions to take steps toward healing and a new life. They may falter and succumb to self-pity or even bitterness. But God in his faithfulness (for he's been there all along) provides the solace and comfort needed, often through the encouragement and love of old friends or family. They know, as Naomi did, that "he will . . . sustain you in your old age" (Ruth 4:15) and they praise God for his faithfulness to the very end.

The Persistent Widow (Luke 18:1–8)

Jesus told the story of a widow—defenseless, helpless, and unprotected. Had she had a male relative, that person would no doubt have advocated for her. Alone, she bravely persisted in pleading with the local judge for justice. In this parable Jesus didn't explain what the woman was advocating for, but he recognized her courage and persistence before the heartless judge who finally relented just to get her off his back.

Today this valiant woman might be advocating for racial justice, for life for the unborn, or for overturning corruption. It is not her dependency or age that strikes us, nor the fact that she is helpless and alone. Rather, we see a woman determined to make a difference in spite of the hard knocks life has given her.

The widow's role in Jewish culture proved difficult if she had no relatives to provide for her. The Old Testament made provision for her care by other family members (Deut. 25:5), but the New Testament put the responsibility ultimately on the church.

"If any woman who is a believer has widows in her family, she should help them and not let the church be burdened with them, so that the church can help those widows who are really in need" (1 Tim. 5:16). Paul laid out strict guidelines as to how to help widows (who obviously had no social security).

"No widow may be put on the list of widows unless she is over sixty, has been faithful to her husband, and is well-known for her good deeds," he instructed Timothy (1 Tim. 5:9–10a).

At the time of Paul's writing, sixty represented an advanced stage in life. Frequent pregnancies and primitive medical care limited a woman's life span. Paul taught that widows should continue serving others (e.g., washing the feet of the saints, helping those in trouble, devoting themselves to all kinds of good deeds) until they were unable to care for themselves. The persistent widow seemed to fulfill these expectations.

She reminds us of our responsibility to advocate for justice. In our senior years we hopefully will have gained credibility, experience, and wisdom to be compassionate spokeswomen for issues of injustice in our world—girls caught in sexual slavery, child pornography on the Internet, and religious intolerance, to name a few.

Jesus and Older Women (Luke 13:10–16)

Jesus taught respect and concern for older women by his deeds rather than his words. Remember the bent-over woman who had suffered from a spinal disease (possibly osteoporosis) for eighteen years? She was probably considered a non-person by the "righteous" worshippers in the synagogue that morning. They didn't give her lonely suffering a second thought.

Standing at the back of the synagogue where women belonged, the woman couldn't see what was happening at the front. Bent over from her waist, she could barely raise her head. Out in the streets her eyes could only see a narrow world of feet and dirt and sometimes children's faces staring into hers as they hurled taunts.

We don't know why she came to the synagogue, for as a woman it was unlikely that she'd been taught the Scriptures or had received encouragement from its leaders. Perhaps she'd heard that this day the healer would be there. Yes! She heard a deep gentle voice reading comforting words from the prophet Isaiah, and she closed her eyes, imagining that they were meant for her.

To her surprise the voice grew louder. "Woman, come up here." Her head swung from one side to the other. What woman was he talking about? There was no other woman around her. Did he mean her? Slowly she shuffled forward, feeling conspicuous, the gnarled walking stick she'd carried these eighteen years steadying her progress. She could imagine the synagogue ruler's look of disdain and displeasure.

A face appeared in her line of vision—a warm, strong face with compassion in his eyes and a hint of a smile around his expressive mouth. He had knelt down before her so she could look into his eyes, and he spoke more softly now, "Woman, you are set free from your infirmity" (Luke 13:12b).

With a firm grip he took her hand and slowly raised her to a standing position. Freed! She was free of the frozen spine and the aching muscles; she could straighten her neck and lift her arms. She stood tall and regal in her ragged robe, her stick clattering to the ground.

Those around began to murmur, and the ruler pontificated, "There are six days for work. So come and be healed on those days, not on the Sabbath" (Luke 13:14b). As if healing were a common occurrence in his life!

Jesus suddenly turned in anger to the crowd: "You hypocrites! Doesn't each of you on the Sabbath untie his ox or donkey from the stall and lead it out to give it water? Then should not this woman, a daughter of Abraham, whom Satan has kept bound for eighteen long years, be set free on the Sabbath day from what bound her?" (Luke 13:15–16).

Jesus is still freeing women today from many kinds of bondage that cripples them. Is something causing you to shuffle bent over and self-effacing? Are you frozen by a lack of self-worth? Have past sins burdened you with shame? Are you taunted by insignificance? Does increasing age weaken your self-image? No matter what deforms our personality or body; no matter our weakness or hopelessness, Jesus will continue to love and care for us until the day he calls us home.

Anna—Persistent in Prayer (Luke 2:36–38)

Anna pursued her passion for prayer and fasting throughout her long life. She became a widow after only seven years of marriage. Since Jewish girls married around fourteen, she was probably only twenty-one when her husband died. Scripture does not make it clear whether she was a widow for eighty-four years, making her 105 years old, or simply eighty-four years of age.

Anna is one of only eight prophetesses listed in Scripture. (Others were Miriam, Deborah, Huldah, and the four daughters of Philip.) This was an extra special calling in Anna's day, for there had been no prophets in Israel, male or female, for hundreds of years.

Life didn't stop for Anna after she became a widow. Rather, she fled to God and dedicated herself to serving him in his temple. Scripture tells us that she spent every day in the temple, praying and fasting. She might have even lived in one of the many rooms of the temple.

As a prophetess, Anna spoke messages from God. She knew the Scriptures well and understood the prophecies concerning the coming Messiah. When Mary and Joseph came into the temple to present their child to God, the Holy Spirit confirmed in her heart that the baby so tenderly carried by this poor couple was the promised One—the One she'd been waiting for. Overwhelmed with joy she ran up to the family, thanking God and calling out to all around her that this was the child who would bring redemption to Jerusalem. How remarkable when we realize that later Jewish religious leaders did not recognize who Jesus was even after seeing his powerful miracles and hearing his divine teaching.

We don't know when Anna began praying full-time in the temple, but the story implies she'd been doing this for a long time. She probably started praying as a young widow, and as the truths of prophecy became clearer, she prayed earnestly that God would allow her to see the coming Messiah. That many others had prayed the same prayer over hundreds of years did not deter her from persistently praying for what God had revealed to her.

Anna modeled what God would like us to strive for as we age—an increasing knowledge of his Word; a growing faith to believe his promises; persistence in prayer; and the ability to speak about his precious Son to all who will listen.

Studies indicate that older women are the primary intercessors in the church. Researcher George Barna finds that women are 16 percent more likely than men to pray and 39 percent more likely to have a devotional or quiet time.[1] Anna didn't wait until she was elderly to start praying. Nor should we!

Like Anna, Joy Dawson, a model of finishing well whose story follows this chapter, began her disciplined prayer life as a young woman. We can learn valuable lessons from her long life of global intercession.

A Biblical Mandate

While this book deals primarily with how to prepare for a fruitful and meaningful rest of our lives, God also expects us to respect and honor those who are our elders. Just as Jesus honored and respected the weak and aged, so we need to practice the same kind of love and compassion to the elders around us. Perhaps there are "nobodies" in our lives who deserve the kind of love Jesus demonstrated.

Moses commanded, "Rise in the presence of the aged, show respect for the elderly and revere your God" (Lev. 19:32). Unfortunately not only today's generation, but as we shall see in chapter two, throughout history, many seem to have lost sight of this teaching.

Joy Dawson

VISION IN THE MIDST OF PAIN

Joy Dawson's Bible-teaching ministry has taken her to fifty-five countries around the world. Multitudes have been blessed by her television and radio ministries, and countless lives have been changed through the distribution of her books and tapes. Crossing denominational lines, the majority of her penetrating teachings are addressed to spiritual leaders. This chapter focuses on her ministry of intercession.

One of the many happy memories of Joy's childhood was the occasional visit from her Aunt Dahlia Manins. Dahlia served as a missionary among the Chinese and Maori minorities in New Zealand. Once every year or two she came back to visit her youngest brother (Joy's father) and his family in Auckland for three months.

Joy had four brothers, but it's understandable that Dahlia, who'd never married because of the call of God on her life, had a special love for her little niece. Joy was the nearest thing to Dahlia's having her own child. Joy experienced a very close bonding with her aunt.

"She loved me to death," Joy explains. "Can't you imagine how this godly intercessor prayed for me, and what an influence she had over my life?"[2] In later years Joy realized that much of her mantle of intense intercession had come as a result of Aunt Dahlia's prayers.

Joy's father was a Bible teacher, evangelist, and pastor who pioneered Christian radio in New Zealand. Both her parents were outstanding soul winners. Sharing the gospel with others became as natural as eating and breathing to their little girl. Family Bible reading and prayer were daily events in their home.

Consistent with her remarkable ministry of hospitality, Joy's mother often invited Jim Dawson to the Maninses' home for a meal after church. Jim enjoyed the camaraderie with the four brothers and their fourteen-year-old sister, Joy.

With New Zealand's entrance into the Second World War, Jim joined the military and was gone for several years. On his return he found Joy had grown into an attractive young woman. At five foot three inches her petite frame exuded energy; her sparkling green eyes twinkled with enthusiasm; and her quick smile reflected an inner beauty. When after several years of growing friendship Jim asked Joy to marry him, she told him two things would have to happen.

"One, God would have to give me a deep-seated, unshakable conviction within my spirit that this was His will for me," she wrote in *Forever Ruined for the Ordinary.* "Two, God would have to cause me to fall in love with him. Well, as I sought God for direction, He really did a number on me on both counts—big-time!"[3]

An Important Revelation

Joy and Jim married in 1948 and settled in their little home on Aldersgate Road in Auckland.

Early in their marriage Jim and Joy attended an Easter convention where an American pastor, Larry Love, was the main speaker. He spoke on the importance of intercession in the life of every believer. Joy already knew that God worked in partnership with believers' prayers to change other people's lives. But she did not have the biblical understanding that

God requires our prayer lives to consistently include a far broader spectrum than those of our personal interests.

Joy returned from that conference with a powerful impression that she could do nothing less than obey what God had shown her. "I heard the Word of the Lord; if Larry Love never did anything else but come to New Zealand for that young wife it was worth it," she declares. She started to intercede for missionaries from her denomination. Though she did not realize it that day, God was going to impact the whole world through her commitment to pray for others.

God's Command

Joy and Jim held a prayer meeting in their home with three evangelists every second Monday. Joy found these protracted times of prayer for lost souls in their city exhilarating. One night as he was leaving, one of the evangelists commented, "As usual we've had a fantastic time in prayer. It was just as great as when I am on my own."

This was a new concept to Joy. She realized that she didn't have to wait until she met with others for inspiration to pray effectively and at length. The very next morning she rushed through her housework and got down on her knees beside her bed, asking God to show her for whom she should pray. To her chagrin she was finished in fifteen minutes. But determined to obey what God had shown her she promised, "I'll be back tomorrow, God, same time.

"I regularly went back to the place of prayer, submitting to the Holy Spirit, believing him to come upon me, to enlarge my prayer life. Persistency, determination, and submission to the Holy Spirit pays off. How do you learn to pray? By praying. There are no excuses for anybody."

Joy continued to enlarge her prayer life, even as her family grew with the birth of their son, John. One morning during her pregnancy, she walked out to the letter-box to get the mail. Walking back along the path to her little home she heard the

Holy Spirit speaking: *You belong to the nations of the world, and as a Christian you are responsible to be praying for the nations of the world.*

This thought had never entered her mind. She'd been praying for people—for the unconverted in her city, for unsaved friends, for missionaries. But for the nations? She'd never heard of anyone speaking of that before. She remembers saying audibly, "You're right. I'll start praying for the nations."

So in childlike obedience, Joy got down on her knees and said, "Which nation do you want me to start praying for, Lord?" And she felt the Holy Spirit directing her to pray for Afghanistan—a place she knew nothing about except that it was in the Middle East. She began praying for the nation and the children of God living there as the Holy Spirit directed.

"Do you get the simplicity of this?" she asks. "I believe the Holy Spirit brings that understanding about our responsibility in prayer for the nations to millions of his children and they do nothing about it. I believe in the ministry of intercession that there are the obedient and the disobedient in relation to what we do with what God says.

"The first six months after I started disciplining myself and earnestly praying for others, my spiritual maturity increased 100 percent. I was receiving God's heart and receiving God's mind for others and that was changing me, just listening to the Holy Spirit. It was exciting. I was totally ruined for the ordinary," Joy asserts.

God's Provision

Though Jim never held Joy back from her new life of prayer, he himself didn't join her personal times of intercession in those early years. By now a daughter had joined their family and he willingly cared for their two children while Joy was on her knees in the bedroom. Most times God would impress upon her the need to intercede when a Bible teacher or evangelist was speaking, and she would disappear for a protracted time. Only these preachers and Jim knew she was doing this.

At this time Joy was frequently speaking to women's groups all over Auckland and surrounding towns and cities within driving distance. While attending a missions conference the Holy Spirit impressed on her to give money to a mission organization. She responded that she had no money, but God's Spirit reminded her that she had a car. She used her little old car to get to her speaking engagements and do the family shopping. If she sold her car how was she going to get there? "That was God's problem," she figured.

As soon as possible she sold the car and wrote a check to the mission. That was a Friday. Fortunately she didn't need a car until Tuesday. On Tuesday morning she was "up to her dandruff" (up to her eyebrows) with a lot of housework when the phone rang. The woman on the other end of the line wanted to come for counseling. Though Joy didn't want to stop her work to counsel she told the woman she would phone her back. She dropped to her knees to ask the Lord what to do. He told her to invite the woman to come.

In the kitchen over lunch preparations the woman encouraged Joy to attend a special meeting across town later in the week. Joy said, "That would be nice, dear, but I don't have a car."

The woman exclaimed, "You don't have a car! So you're the one to whom I'm supposed to give my car!" She went on to explain that she was going away as a missionary (to the exact organization to which Joy had given the money) and had been looking for someone to keep her car. God provided a much better car because of her steps of obedience.

Prayer Partners

In one of her morning prayer times, God impressed upon Joy to call Shelagh McAlpine and ask her to become a prayer partner. Shelagh had four children and Joy had two, and they arranged their schedules so that they could meet on Thursday afternoons to pray for the nations. They prayed every Thursday for two years before Shelagh returned to England where she began the Lydia Movement, which eventually enlisted women all over the world to pray for the nations.

After Shelagh left, Joy began praying with two other close friends, Dorothy Leonard and Hazel Elliott. They met for years every other week starting in the morning and for most of the afternoon, waiting on God, listening, praying for peoples and nations. "Out of that came the ten principles for effective intercession, which have been distributed all over the world, on cards, in magazines and books," Joy recalls. (See appendix C.)

The three partners saw many miraculous answers to prayer. During the uprising in the Congo during the sixties, they were directed to pray for a woman missionary who had been reported missing and presumed murdered.

"It was a real step of faith just to speak her name, let alone continue in prayer for her. However, direction to pray for her life to be spared and for her protection came to us from specific Scriptures quickened by the Holy Spirit as we continued to diligently seek God,"[4] Joy wrote.

Joy and her friends believed the missionary's life would be saved. Even after the press announced her death, they continued to wait quietly for a reversal of the news. Weeks later they learned that the missionary had been rescued by three nuns who had hidden her and cared for her until she could be returned to her coworkers. The woman's rescue had occurred the very day they were interceding for her deliverance!

Joy continued to regularly pray with and for others while she opened her home to guests, many of whom were spiritual leaders. One Baptist minister stayed at their home while speaking in a local church. He had been praying with Joy for an extended time in intercession one morning. Before he left for the meeting that night she asked if he would like them to pray again. Joy recalls with a chuckle, "He looked at me and said, 'Joy, I really think I've done enough praying today!' Well he was probably right. I'm just a fanatic on prayer."

After Joy was filled with the Holy Spirit, she developed an intense desire to know God, the author of the Bible. Though she had never attended Bible school, she seriously studied the Word of God each day. Over the years Joy studied the character and ways of God, developing her own personal concordance of many hundreds of verses related to those subjects.

"I would sometimes be five hours in a day while the children were away at school just poring over the Scriptures, studying the character and ways of God," she says. Her excellent memory enabled her to memorize countless Scriptures and where they are found, a valuable asset in her Bible teaching and extensive evangelism ministry.

The Stage Is Set

Although Joy was regularly bringing the Word of the Lord to women's meetings, the doors to meetings with men in attendance were closed because of her gender. However, in 1967 a spiritual leader who understood Joy's teaching gift and who believed she had a message everyone should hear, invited her to speak at a convention attended by both men and women. One of the speakers was Loren Cunningham, founder of a new and little-known mission, Youth With A Mission (YWAM).

After the convention the Dawsons invited Loren to stay in their home. "He was very interested in the way I prayed, which was waiting on God, listening in silence, asking the Holy Spirit to tell me what to say, not praying until I heard and then speaking out what he said," she explains. They had many discussions about kingdom-related issues, and before Loren left for his home in the United States he asked for a tape of any of Joy's teachings, which she gave him without another moment's thought.

To her surprise Loren returned to New Zealand a year later with invitations for Joy from pastors in the United States to come and speak in their churches. Initially Joy thought he was joking. No one knew this little housewife from Auckland. But Loren assured her the invitation was real. He also asked her to teach in YWAM's first school of evangelism in Switzerland. After much seeking from God, both Jim and Joy were directed to tell Loren the answer was "yes."

By the next year, when God released her to leave home, leaders in five other nations had invited Joy. Though no one offered to pay her fare, God miraculously provided her seven-nation ticket. Obediently seeking God's will, Joy determined which of the many invitations she should accept.

A New Role for Jim

Joy was being asked to teach both men and women. Providentially Jim had been doing some study of the Scriptures on this very topic. God started to unfold the concept of equality to him in the Book of Genesis. Jim had peace and a growing conviction in his heart that his wife was living in purity and holiness and in obedience to God. As a man who is called to love his wife as Christ loved the church, he wanted her to be fulfilled. Joy recalls, "He released me with the deep conviction in his heart that what I was doing was right—that he had a partial revelation, but not full, about some difficult Scriptures that Paul wrote."

Joy admits that she herself didn't have an explanation. All she knew was: "If you're submitted to the Holy Spirit and you love God's Word and there are portions of the Scripture which you can't understand, he in time will give you or others insights to those difficult Scriptures. He'll show you how there's no conflict between his voice and his written word."

In the years ahead comprehensive biblical research by many evangelical authors have more than confirmed Joy's call to teach his Word to men and women.

Providentially God had led Jim to change jobs to one with more flexible hours so that he could care for their two teenage children for three months while Joy traveled in seven countries, speaking morning and night.

After nine months at home, Joy took a second overseas speaking tour of more than three months. Then the Lord stirred

Jim and Joy's hearts for him to leave secular employment, and they joined YWAM as unsalaried missionaries.

"The stirrings from the Holy Spirit continued unabated," Joy says. "At this time for three whole weeks I kept hearing in my spirit a verse of Scripture I had memorized: 'For God is at work in you, both to will and to work for his good pleasure' (Phil. 2:13 RSV). At first I wondered why these impressions persisted, until I came to the understanding that it was God's way of saying to us that it was God who was stirring us, putting these thoughts and desires into our hearts, preparing us to take the big step of obedience and faith to become lifetime missionaries to the nations. Clear scriptural directions were also given to us both."

This meant leaving their home, family, and friends and taking their two teenagers to California where YWAM was based, without any promised financial support.

Jim drew on his years in business to become the administrator of the little YWAM office that at that time had only three staff members, and today counts seventeen thousand missionaries in its worldwide ministry. As the mission grew, God changed Jim's ministry to International Staff Pastor.

"Then God changed that again," Joy explains, "and caused him to be like the knife and the fork with me. In the ministry God has given me, I cannot do what I do without my husband. We do everything together; we have a united ministry. He looks after our business side. He does all the computer work while I do the book writing and teaching . . . and we're joined together in one ministry of evangelism, counseling, and intercession. Jim is my wonderful prayer partner."

Over Thirty Years of Global Ministry

Joy's ministry of international teaching blossomed in the years ahead. She traveled frequently, often without Jim, to difficult places like Egypt and Afghanistan and eventually to fifty-five countries. She directed the majority of her teaching to spiritual leaders both in YWAM and at many interdenominational leadership conferences worldwide. Loren Cunningham had released her right from the beginning to minister to the body of Christ wherever she was called.

Joy has written five books, including *Intercession, Thrilling and Fulfilling,* and *Forever Ruined for the Ordinary: The Adventure of Hearing and Obeying God's Voice.* Her booklets and tapes have been distributed around the globe.

Joy rejoices that both her children have a heart for the world. After serving the mission since he was nineteen years old, John became the president of YWAM International in 2003. His three sons are also missionaries. Jill had a passion for missions from her childhood and she, her husband, and two children also serve with YWAM.

The Road Becomes Rough

One night in mid-February 1993 Joy awoke with lower back pain like she'd never had before. She describes her initial response to God: "First I said, 'Bring the maximum glory to your name through this pain, in whichever way you choose.' Second I asked, 'Reveal to me the purposes and/or the causes of this pain.' Then, 'Show me everything you're trying to teach me.' And finally, 'Tell me the next thing you want me to do. Thank you for the answers in your way and time.'" Four months later God spoke clearly to her from the Book of Job that she was in a time of severe testing.

In the months ahead Joy pursued every form of medical advice, but the pain increased. After diligently seeking God's clear direction Joy had major back surgery, one year after the pain surfaced. But instead of getting relief, she was much worse, with a severely damaged nervous system in addition. It took two years of an intense trial of faith before Joy was able to resume any form of normal life or public ministry.

Joy believes, "Undoubtedly the revelation of God's character and the understanding of his way that I had studied for decades was the main reason that I was able to maintain a life of worship, thankfulness, and praise plus intercession for others."

When I interviewed her at age seventy-six (ten years after her initial pain) she was somewhat better, though the debilitating pain persists. Jim does the driving while she lies elevated in the backseat of the car. Her public speaking is now limited, but God has told her to write books as her main ministry, next to worship, witnessing, and intercession.

Joy rejoices in the unfailing character of God even when his ways are past finding out.

"One of the most precious things that has come out of all the suffering has been the way God has consistently spoken to Jim and me through his Word, that as I endure this pain and perplexity with patience and faith, he will supernaturally heal me in his way and time. I live with the certain expectancy," Joy testifies.

"I only want the timing to be when my precious Savior can get the maximum glory to his wonderful name. This assurance, plus God's amazing grace, along with the prayers of many faithful intercessors, enables me to live above the trial, mentally, emotionally, and spiritually."

Watching her sparkling eyes and animated expression as she declares her confidence in God, one would never know that she was in pain.

Through it all Joy found her greatest comfort and satisfaction in her intimate relationship with God. For years she and Jim have had a prayer meeting almost every night.

"I believe that the kingdom of God is extended more through the ministry of intercession than any other ministry. I have that vision and conviction, so it's a priority with us," she declares.

Joy maintains that there are no excuses to keep us from the ministry of intercession. She has prayed fervently alone; regularly in groups with Christian leaders; with two or three other women; with her precious life partner; and with countless others as opportunities have arisen.

"It's no wonder that I feel more fulfilled after an effective time of intercession than after I have preached a message," Joy claims. "When I speak to people about God I have no guarantee they will act upon the truths I've spoken. But when I pray to God about people, I know he'll always act in response to my cries as I pray according to his ways from his Word."

"If all our other faculties were taken from us and all we had left was a sound mind and a beating heart, we could still be mightily used of God to affect the history of the nations through the marvelous ministry of intercession,"[5] Joy says. And that's exactly what she plans to do until God calls her home.

Aging through the Ages

There is an old Arab saying that when each child is born,
it is surrounded by one hundred angels. For every year a
male lives, an angel is added; for every year a female lives,
an angel dies.

Elizabeth Markson, *Handbook on Women and Aging*

What do you feel are the worst things about aging? In a questionnaire I sent out to Christian women over fifty years old a surprising number responded "none" to that question. Many liked their status in life just fine. They gave the highest negative response—50 percent—to "feeling tired and lacking energy."[1]

Older women, however, have long been the brunt of uncomplimentary stories and have been accused of evil intent. We all heard fairy stories about the "wicked old witch" in our childhood. Remember the gnarled old woman in the gingerbread cottage who enticed Hansel and Gretel into her home and hopefully into her oven? Or the wicked fairy godmother who condemned Sleeping Beauty to death at the prick of a spindle?

When Women Were Maligned

The wicked old witch, unfortunately, existed as more than just a figment of our imagination. In the Middle Ages Europe became the breeding ground for witch-hunts. Historians believe that the wars, epidemics, and even the cultural upheaval during the Reformation lay the groundwork and opened the way for accusations against suspected witches.

During the height of the mass hysteria that occurred from 1550 to 1650 A.D. an estimated forty to fifty thousand executions took place, twenty-six thousand in Germany alone. Women made up 80 percent of those accused and convicted. Historian Brian P. Levack writes, "The limited data we have regarding the age of witches . . . shows a solid majority of witches were older than fifty, which in the early modern period was considered to be a much more advanced age than today."[2]

A growing misogyny permeated the culture. Childless older women often fell outside the care of the patriarchal family. Without a recognized place in society and often poor and begging, these women became easy targets of accusations of witchcraft.

In that same era the theologian John Calvin taught that the physical, mental, and moral deterioration in old age was punishment for sin, yet paradoxically he believed the "pious aged should be honored as visible monuments of God's grace."[3]

Why did the witch-hunt spread to Salem, Massachusetts, in the late seventeenth century? No one really knows. Some feel it had political undertones as the local church split over property and bad feelings emerged between families. Others believe that the two teenage girls who initially accused a neighbor and a black servant of witchcraft were simply bored and made up stories about seeing apparitions and visions related to the accused. The accusations snowballed, and twenty-five predominantly older women accused of being witches were hung in Salem and neighboring towns in 1692.

Women's Roles in Early America

In spite of isolated witch-hunts, families generally respected and took responsibility for their elders in colonial America. Three and four generations lived together in an extended family with grandmothers caring for children and performing whatever tasks they could manage, filling a needed role in the household.

The whole family worked together as a unit, tending fields and livestock and making products to sell or barter. Women's roles remained primarily within the household, and older women continued to work as long as they were physically able.

The nineteenth-century Victorians saw a growing middle and upper class that continued to shelter and care for older women within the family unit. The romanticized Victorian household considered women of all ages as fragile and needing protection from the harsh realities of life. Excessive modesty, proper decorum, and social class distinctions ruled the behavior for women fortunate enough to live in these comfortable circumstances.

Women in the Workforce

With the Industrial Revolution in the nineteenth century came a societal change that affected women of all ages. Family cottage industries found it more and more difficult to survive as new machines in factories supplanted work done in the home. For the first time in history women and children left their homes by the droves to work twelve to fourteen hours a day in sweatshops, earning barely enough to keep body and soul together. The upper middle class owners and managers had the means to enjoy the benefits of having grandmother, mother, and children safe and comfortable in a sheltered environment. Though some widows were able to take over a family business after their husbands died, women generally could not own property.

But for those in less fortunate circumstances, every able-bodied person in an urban family had to find work outside the home, often in dangerous and unhealthy conditions. Women and children were paid the lowest wages without benefits of time off for illness. Many a mother returned to work within a day of delivering her baby, for she could not afford to lose one day's income. Reports tell of women working in the mines, stripped to their waist because of the heat. Records in Britain from this period indicate that some women as old as sixty and seventy worked in factories for three or four shillings a day.

The indigent without families or those unable to work ended up in the "poorhouse," a Dickensian symbol of corruption and brutality.

Grand Old Ladies Taking Risks

In the midst of societal and economic problems, a rising women's movement developed to speak against alcoholism among men, which had grown to epidemic proportions. Now, at the end of long hours in sometimes dark and dangerous sweatshops, men spent their evenings and meager earnings in the taverns.

Out of this destructive scene rose the prohibition movement, whose most vocal and influential leaders were women. Carrie Nation entered taverns, smashing bottles and mirrors before she delivered her evangelistic messages. Her iconoclasm was based on the conviction that God had called her. "We wanted God to save their souls, and give us ability and opportunity to destroy this soul damning business."[4]

As a Quaker, Susan B. Anthony approached the issue with less violence but no less fervor. She worked to bring about prohibition and formed the first women's temperance movement. Anthony became the leading voice in the call for women's right to vote and remained active until her eightieth year. She died in 1906, fourteen years before the passage of the 19th Amendment, granting women the right to vote.

One of Anthony's contemporaries, Francis Willard, founded the WCTU (Women's Christian Temperance Union), the largest nineteenth-century women's organization. She soon realized that laws prohibiting alcohol would be passed only if women had the ballot. She became an active suffragette after an encounter with God while on her knees in prayer. She wrote, "There was borne in upon my mind, as I believe from loftier regions, this declaration, 'You are to speak for woman's ballot as a weapon for protection for her home.'"[5]

Though many younger women joined the suffragette cause, pictures of their activities and stories of courage and persistence reveal that older women felt strongly enough about these issues to risk their reputations and comforts for a cause to which they believed God had called them.

Financial Security for Women

In spite of improvements in working conditions and the right to vote, women in the early 1900s had little financial security. The crash of 1929 put millions of men and women out of work with no safety net; the jobless rate reached almost 25 percent. In 1935 President Franklin D. Roosevelt initiated the Social Security Act, insuring that every wage earner, man or woman, would have some financial assistance after his or her retirement.

Two provisions of the Social Security Act affected the senior years of women. One is the idea of enforced retirement at age sixty-five. Prior to 1935 there was no such thing as retirement; people worked as long as they could and depended on their families to care for them when they could no longer work. The mandatory retirement age of sixty-five eased older people out of the workplace—and in essence forced them into lives of consumption and uselessness.

Second, married women receive half of their husband's social security benefits even if they have never worked outside the home. As widows they may continue to receive their husband's benefits, granting them some financial security.

The Situation Globally

Certainly a senior woman in America fares better than her counterpart in developing countries where older women make up the poorest of the poor. Only 18 percent of developing countries provide any kind of social security benefits.

In some African tribes when a woman becomes a widow she loses status as well as her property. Her in-laws may simply confiscate everything she owns, leaving her and her children destitute. Economists say that in the next two or three decades there will be three times as many poor older women in developing countries as there are now.

An increasing number of poverty-stricken older women care for the poorest and most vulnerable—children whose parents died of AIDS and who themselves may be infected. In 2002 more than five million adults out of a population of twenty-six million lived with HIV-AIDS in sub-Saharan countries, and life expectancy dropped below forty.[6] In several sub-Saharan countries half of new mothers will die of AIDS, increasing the burden on extended family members and elderly grannies.

Adult children in many developing countries such as China highly respect and care for their elderly parents, though with the rise of capitalism and urbanization this becomes more difficult. Some years ago the Singapore government berated young couples for not taking their elderly parents into their homes and caring for them as tradition called for.

Even primitive people such as the Stone Age tribes of West Irian Jaya in the highlands of New Guinea provided their elderly with a house and a pig to keep them warm on cold nights. However, "just 150 miles away from West Irian Jaya, villagers bury their old alive."[7]

Ageism in America

In spite of advances in financial and educational opportunities for women in America, stereotyping remains. Ask young people what comes into their minds when they think of a sixty-five-year-old woman and you may hear things like:

- someone in poor health with aches and pains
- losing it mentally, even senile
- slow
- resistant to change, out of touch
- poor
- nonproductive
- shuffles, bent over

Pulitzer Prize–winning author Robert N. Butler described this attitude as "ageism" when he wrote in 1975, "Ageism can be seen as a process of systematic stereotyping of and discrimination against people because they are old, just as racism and sexism accomplish this with skin color and gender. Old people are categorized as senile, rigid in thought and manner, old-fashioned in morality and skills. . . . Ageism allows the younger generations to see older people as different from themselves; thus they subtly cease to identify with their elders as human beings."[8]

An ad printed in a major news magazine by a nationally known banking chain states, "You can't choose your relatives." It pictures a double-chinned older woman with huge horn-rimmed glasses, wearing a garish print dress and matching turban over straggling gray hair. In her hand she holds a fat, juicy sausage ready to pop into her large open mouth. You can almost hear her booming voice. Is this kind of stereotyping of older women one of the reasons we try to appear younger than our chronological age?

What are some of the messages we receive in our culture today?

1. Youthfulness is best. Whether in ads, television, or catalogues, a whole industry promotes youthful appearance by removing wrinkles, coloring gray hair, strengthening sagging abs, and wearing youthful styles. It's okay to be old if you look young, especially younger than fifty. A woman's essence lies in her youthfulness.

One of the women's catalogues I receive features clothing suitable for more mature bodies—generally more modest than usual. It offers double-knit pull-on pants and cardigans a teenager wouldn't be seen dead in. The styles appeal to a more conservative, older clientele, but of the hundred or so models only one could possibly be as old as forty. The rest have slim, shapely, bronzed bodies with no sagging "chicken wing" arms or bulbous hips. Yet this catalogue advertises sizes as large as 3X. Can it be we are to imagine ourselves looking that glamorous and youthful in these clothes?

2. Seniors don't have to age. Increasingly, many companies are advertising denture creams, heartburn medicine, bladder control pills, arthritis pain relievers, and osteoporosis prevention. Couples who take their age-renewing vitamins are seen sailing happily on a choppy sea or screaming in delight on a whirling ride at an amusement park, once again able to do what they did thirty years ago. These ads present an unrealistic picture of our senior years.

Some years ago a magazine for older women was launched with attractive seniors on the cover. Editors soon received complaints that their audience preferred models of younger women. Readers saw themselves as looking fifteen years younger than their actual age, and the staff quickly changed its image.

3. Seniors' opinions have little value. Few strong, leading film or TV characters play the part of an older woman (Angela Lansbury in *Murder She Wrote* was one exception). But when *Wall Street Week* dumped market-analyst Louis Rukeyser because the average age of his audience was sixty-two, editorial writer Dale McFeatters took notice. With tongue in cheek he warned, "It's time people sixty and over struck back. . . . The sixty-plussers could force cancellation of any youth-oriented show simply by watching it in large numbers. Advertisers pin their hopes on demographics. Catch the attention of the eighteen- to thirty-four-year-olds, the advertisers' favorite age group, and they'll become your followers. Never mind that the mean net worth of a family headed by someone between sixty-five and seventy-four in 2002 was $465,500, while for under thirty-five it was $65,900."[9]

While riding on a bus I overheard an elderly couple discuss a phone call from a TV rating company. When the woman said that she was seventy-five, the caller responded, "Please tell me you're not that old. You were to be my last call for the night." Evidently rating companies don't like to talk to anyone over sixty-five.

4. Seniors are unproductive. When speaking about the growing senior population, comments about being unproductive or surplus are generally held privately or behind closed doors. After all, seniors command a powerful vote. Sixty-seven percent of people over sixty-five voted in the presidential election in 2000 while only 24 percent voted among the twenty- to twenty-four-year olds.[10] Conscious of the demands of seniors when it comes to social security, prescription drugs, and Medicare, Congress carefully considers the desires of this powerful voting bloc.

Yet occasionally someone will unwittingly let the cat out of the bag, like the doctor commenting on *60 Minutes* about an expensive medical advance. He questioned the use of the procedure on older people saying, "What's the value of their life? They're not working anymore."

Contrast this with the anguish of Rosalynn Carter's mother who, when forced to retire from the post office at age seventy cried, "No one thinks I can do good work anymore." Mrs. Carter went on to say that her mother soon found another job in a flower shop.[11]

During the Carter administration Rosalynn lobbied for the Age Discrimination Act, which eliminated mandatory retirement in the federal government and raised the age from sixty-five to seventy in the private sector.

In 2000, television writers filed a class action suit against TV networks, studios, and production companies with age discrimination, claiming a silent conspiracy in Hollywood.

It seems the industry believes that anyone over forty can't understand the youth culture; two-thirds of prime-time series did not employ one writer over fifty.

The Equal Employment Opportunity Commission receives more than sixteen thousand age discrimination cases a year. Unfortunately, "Modern progress lowers the value of older people at the same time as it adds years to our lives. The longer we live the less we are worth, and we *will* live longer."[12]

Paradoxically while retirement and discrimination force older people (and some not so old) to quit working, society tends to call them nonproductive and a drain on the economy. Many older people thumb their noses at this observation by speeding along the highways in their expensive motor homes with the slogan blazoned on the back, "We're spending our children's inheritance."

The image of being useless and nonproductive has persisted. Dr. I. L. Nascher, who coined the term *geriatrics* in 1909, spent his whole life trying to improve care for the aged. He wrote, "We realize that for all practical purposes the lives of the aged are useless, that they are often a burden to themselves, their family and the community at large."[13] When Nascher made this statement social security had not even been thought of. Today society fears that social security will not be able to care for the millions of seniors, including the fast-aging baby boomers, who will be drawing on it.

5. Older people lose mental acuity and creativity as they age. My husband often tells a favorite joke when he forgets something:

> Two couples were playing bridge. While the women went into the kitchen to fix food, Chuck leaned over to Jim and said, "You're playing much better tonight. You're remembering every card. What happened?"
>
> Jim responded, "I went to a memory school and it's really helped me."
>
> "What was the name of the school?" Chuck asked.
>
> Jim asked him, "What's the name of that flower with thorns?"

"A rose," Chuck responded.

Jim called back to the kitchen, "Rose, what's the name of that school I went to about memory?"

Many believe that older people lose mental capacities as they age. Employers hesitate to hire older workers, fearing that they won't be able to learn new procedures.

A generally held theory declares that the brain loses size and weight over the years, that brain cells do not rejuvenate, that short-term memory fades, and that creativity declines with age. While some of this may be true, we will see in chapter 3 that our brain has an amazing capacity to learn and remember and that some of the most creative people in the world did their best work after age seventy. Not only does society endorse the belief that seniors' brain capacity diminishes, but as we age, we ourselves accept the stigma.

We are embarrassed every time we forget a name; we hesitate to attend classes for fear we will disgrace ourselves; we don't attempt to be creative, convinced that we are inadequate.

Poor Self-Image

We unwittingly draw in our culture's stereotypes from the media, from what we read and hear, or from our own experiences. We absorb these attitudes into our soul like paper towels mopping up a spill.

I was shocked at how easily I had imbibed this message that I represented the stereotype when I attended a social evening at the home of people I'd never met. I knew only the person who'd invited me. After initial brief introductions, she left me to interact and joke with the others; though the guests were polite they paid little attention to me. I listened and forced myself to laugh at appropriate times, but I felt as invisible as a SARS virus.

As the evening wore on, various guests dutifully asked me, "Where are you from?" or "What church do you attend?"

They never asked me what I did or anything personal. I felt like a little old lady who'd escaped from a nursing home, with emphasis on the *old* since everyone else was younger. I sensed that they didn't think I had much to contribute to their conversation.

I wanted to interrupt their talk of recipes and cars and tell them of my years of mission work in Africa, of the books I'd written, or about my two children serving as missionaries in a Muslim country. Would their perception of me have changed? Would I have had my identity back, feeling affirmed by those around me?

Sadly I had to admit that my self-image as well as others' perception of me depended on what I had accomplished and where I'd been. I was reminded that ego is at the root of a poor self-image.

As we grow older we project less and less of the outward attributes that spell success. Our physical bodies grow weak and fail us; our beauty fades; our important roles disappear until we wonder what is left. We feel unloved and as valueless as an eight-track tape recorder.

Of course, things can get worse. A woman dying in a nursing home of end-stage cancer wrote this in her diary:

> I want to tell you about one good trade. It has been the hardest one by far. It's ongoing. I had to trade in my old definition of ME. I thought I WAS my abilities; my job; the amount of money I made; the highest degree I earned; the way I looked; the way I cooked; the presents I gave.
>
> I had to figure out that those things aren't me. They are part of my life and losing them counts, but they are not ME. The girl God made is that stripped down substance/soul underneath all those things. I had to figure out how to be brave enough to let that be enough. Be ME—ungiftwrapped. . . .
>
> The first time I got so weak from chemo that I couldn't feed myself, I thought I would come completely undone. My personal dignity was so tangled up with my ability to control my body and its functions. . . . I cared so much about what the person

holding the spoon thought of me. It is still hard for me to trade down, and I fight to keep as much control of my life as I can, but at least some of the time, I can remember what part is really me. . . .

I am glad I have had the time to learn the things that dying has taught me. I'm closer to being an authentic person than I would have been without this. Right now I am not so much worried about taking my last breath. I'm more worried about having the emotional stamina to stay real all the way to the end. I pray for that.[14]

God validates us as women of worth right to the very end of our lives, for he created us in his image. Only after God created woman out of man did he evaluate "all that he had made, and it was very good" (Gen. 1:31a). We worship him for his powerful and glorious creation and for his unlimited love and grace; we worship him because we are his blood children and we bear his genes, his DNA.

God created these marvelous bodies of ours, each one diverse from the other, and we are his beloved in spite of our wrinkles and bulges. Just as God loves and values youth (which in its early stages is a consumer rather than a producer), so he loves and values us as we age, regardless of how we may appear to others and how unproductive we may seem to have become. Hold this precious promise in your heart when you feel unattractive or invisible: "The Lord does not look at the things people look at. Human beings look at the outward appearance, but the Lord looks at the heart" (1 Sam. 16:7 NIV).

The more we know our Creator, the more we'll recognize the "family qualities" we reflect. Our worth rests in what he values, and he has valued us enough to send his Son in the flesh to die for us. The fact that God took on flesh implies the high value he gives to the physical body—in the full freshness of life as well as the weakness of death. "Therefore we do not lose heart. Though outwardly we are wasting away, yet inwardly we are being renewed day by day" (2 Cor. 4:16).

Though the stereotypes had been rattling through my brain the whole evening at that social get-together, I finally took the initiative and began talking to one of the women whose daughter is working in another state. She shared her worry that her daughter wasn't attending church and had no Christian friends. I was able to tell her of a recent answer to prayer when one of my granddaughters for whom I'd been praying for several years submitted herself to Christ. I'd been praying for a Christian friend for her, and it was through this very means that God brought her into fellowship with himself. The woman and I parted with a warm sense that we had touched on something meaningful to both of us. I still don't know what she does for a living, nor does she know what I've done.

In the following model of finishing well we meet Eliza Davis George, a feisty African-American, who did not allow any of society's biases to squelch her passion for God even at ninety-nine years of age.

Eliza Davis George

> Her passion for taking the liberating message of Christ into interior Liberia kept Eliza Davis George serving well into her ninth decade. She lived what she believed, that it's always too soon to quit.

When the villagers heard where Mother Eliza was going they tried to discourage her. "Mother, you shouldn't pass that way—that's the devil bush. One man went there one day and tried to make a farm, and after three days he just died, and nobody knows how he died. Mother Eliza, you shouldn't go."

With the warning ringing in her ears, Eliza and her friend Otto plodded through the thick bush. Only the swish of Otto's cutlass as he cleared a path or the buzz of the flies around their heads broke the hot silence. Otto was leading her to a "cursed place," an area in the interior of Liberia where no villager would farm. As they neared the spot, the ground began to rise slightly so that when Otto said, "This is it," they were standing on the heavily forested crest of a small knoll, with virgin jungle spread out before them and a murky creek pulsing over submerged logs along the bottom of the knoll.

Otto asked once more, "Mother, are you sure you want to build a mission on this land?"

Eliza's confident reply was, "Son, there is no place where God has told us not to stay. This is going to be my life's work. We're not going to move anywhere else."

Standing there on the little knoll with only the birds and insects as witnesses, Mother Eliza Davis George dedicated the land that was to become a lasting monument to God's grace and her persistence to serve him in Liberia.

At seventy-two, she had already spent more than thirty-seven years among the tribal people of Liberia, telling them of the living Christ, planting churches, training thousands of children in her simple mud and thatch schools, and sending her spiritual children even farther into the interior as missionaries.

"We Have Enough Africa over Here"

Her call that day sounded as clear as it had back in 1911 when she shared it with the president of Central Texas College where she served as matron. She could still hear him remonstrate, "Oh please, Miss Davis, don't let yourself get carried away by that foolishness. You don't have to go over there to be a missionary—we have enough Africa over here."

From a practical standpoint her vision had been somewhat far-fetched. As the daughter of former slaves, she knew of no black woman who had gone to Africa from her state of Texas. She was still helping three of her six brothers and sisters through school. When she applied to the General Baptist Convention of Texas, the state president told her, "Miss Davis, you don't have the money, and we ministers stand between you and the people to keep you from getting the money." But Eliza stood her ground. Deep down her heart responded, "But you don't stand between me and my God."

Over the next few months one of the convention leaders introduced her to black churches in Houston, New Orleans, and other places. Word finally came that she had sufficient funds to sail from New York for Liverpool on December 12,

1913, to open a mission with another black missionary, Miss Susie Taylor.

Standing by the rail with Dr. Jordan, a convention leader who had accompanied her to New York, a terrifying thought suddenly struck Eliza. Putting her hand on his arm, she asked, "Dr. Jordan, how must I begin my work when I get to Africa?"

"Any way you can, my dear," he replied as he turned and walked down the gangplank.

An Unexpected Solution

Susie and Eliza started a new mission school in the interior, several miles from the town of Fortesville. They supervised building a mud and thatch house, started Liberian-style farming, and began to teach school. By 1916 they were well established and several hundred villagers had accepted the Christian message.

Then the devastating news struck. The Baptist convention from Texas had split from the National Baptists who sent word that they would replace Eliza with one of their own workers. Months dragged by as Eliza pled with God for direction, crying out, "God, you sent me here. I am not under their orders, I'm under yours, and I won't leave until you tell me to go."

Eliza would never have chosen the answer she received. On a visit to Fortesville to pick up supplies, she met with friends who introduced her to G. Thompson George, originally from British Guyana, who had worked all over Africa. He once visited the grave of David Livingston's wife, and while standing at the grave site the desire to be a missionary in Africa filled his heart.

Mr. George impressed Eliza with his broad knowledge and wide travel experience. But as she scurried through the town to fulfill her errands she put the encounter out of her mind. What a shock to receive a letter from him just two days later asking her to marry him. She had never desired to marry and certainly didn't love Mr. George.

Eliza wrote right back making it clear she had no interest in marriage:

Dear Mr. George:

Thank you for your letter which was delivered to me this morning. I am returning it together with the picture you enclosed. I feel I must explain that had I the desire to marry, I would have done so before leaving America. I didn't come here to marry. I came here to work for the salvation of the souls of these natives, and nothing will deter me from my course.

Your sister in Christ, Eliza L. Davis

But in the months ahead Mr. George persisted, especially when it became clear that Eliza was going to have to leave Africa if she could not find another place to work. Susie had already returned to the States because of recurring malaria, and now the Convention informed Eliza that her replacements at the mission would arrive in August 1917. She had nowhere to go but home.

Once again Mr. George pressed his point, "Miss Davis, I know you refused me once, but things have changed. Unless you find someone to help you, the Convention will force you to leave Africa. We could really work together well; you are a trained teacher with a wonderful way with the natives. I've had years of experience among them and know what it's like to exist in the rugged interior. Won't you let me go and try to find a place for a mission?"

In desperation, as if to get rid of him, she blurted out, "All right, Mr. George, you take my letter to the authorities requesting permission to begin work in Sinoe County. And, if they agree," she heard herself saying, "I'll marry you."

A Strange Partnership

When he returned with an agreement for seventy-five acres of land to start a mission school, Mr. George held her to her promise. Though she didn't love this little man with his English accent and his vast experience, she did respect and admire him. He was a fine Christian and so intelligent. And he *was* offering her the only hope to remain in Africa.

Reaching out to touch him for the first time, Eliza put her hand on his arm and said, "Well, all right, Mr. George. I did make the plan and you did your part. I believe God has shown me that I should marry you."

Eliza kept her promise. For twenty-two years the Georges worked together at Kelton Mission in Sinoe County among the primitive tribes farther in the interior, many of whom had never heard the name of Jesus before. Eliza rejoiced whenever she was able to rescue a little girl whose parents had given her in marriage to an old man and train her at the mission school.

Discouragement and financial disaster plagued the Georges as they worked hard alongside their students doing the back-breaking work it took to farm in Liberia. Eliza began what became her practice through her many years in Africa. She called the children together for singing and prayers three times a day no matter what they were doing or where they were. Her clear voice rang out across the station as she sang one of the old hymns such as "Jesus, Keep Me Near the Cross," and the children would join in singing as they gathered around her.

Several times during those years the Georges traveled to the U.S. to raise support. They found fund-raising difficult in black churches, and their trips sometimes lasted five or six years. Upon their return they would find the mission buildings destroyed from the rampages of insects and incessant rain and their students scattered.

Somehow they weathered their less than ideal marriage. The "children" remember frequent arguments. One morning in January 1939 Mr. George determined to walk to Greenville (twenty-six miles away, at the coast) for some supplies; Eliza tried in vain to stop him.

All through the day Eliza went about her business fighting a nagging fear so unlike her. When darkness fell she could stand the suspense no longer. She sent two of the boys off toward the nearest town, thinking that perhaps Father George had come that far and decided to spend the night.

Eliza spent the next few hours on her knees, praying for her husband (and no doubt for herself), wondering where she had failed him and why he had chosen the path that he had.

Toward midnight she heard voices above the night sounds of the jungle and hurried out to see a procession coming out of the bush, lighting their way with lanterns. Instinctively she knew what they had come to tell her.

The facts were stark and harsh; there was no way to soften the blow. Father had died in the home of a lady friend in Greenville, apparently of a sudden heart attack. With no embalming system, Liberia's heat necessitated burying the corpse within twenty-four hours. When Eliza asked some of the villagers to dig a grave on the mission, they insisted that she give them their usual payment of cane juice. With her utter distaste for the imbibing of liquor, which had become one of Father George's problems, Eliza indignantly sent them away. Instead she took her turn with some of the older mission boys to dig her husband's grave.

Time to Retire?

Over the next six years many of Eliza's dreams came true. She had been able to open four substations farther in the interior and sent out pastors trained at Kelton. Two of her Liberian "daughters," Maude and Cerella, whom she had taken to the U.S., had completed their education and were planning to return to work in Liberia.

One day she received a letter that two of the Baptist Convention's officials, Dr. Redder and Mrs. Fuller, were going to visit them in Liberia. What a time of preparation as Eliza and the children scrubbed, polished, and cooked to give the guests a warm and boisterous African welcome.

When the excitement died down and the villagers returned to their homes, Eliza, Maude, and the Convention leaders began their discussions. Eliza wondered what they had in mind, for she sensed that they were holding something back from her.

Mrs. Fuller insisted that Eliza come home for a rest. "You've been here for ten years, Mother, without a vacation of any kind. With Maude and Cerella here to help you, this is a good time for you to come back."

After a lengthy discussion, Eliza reluctantly agreed, feeling pressured like dough in a cookie press. But after two days at sea Dr. Reeder explained the true purpose of the trip. "Maude felt that it would be very difficult to work under you, especially since she has been well-educated and has new ideas. She is concerned about you. You have labored in Africa for thirty-two years under very difficult conditions. You've had malaria over and over; the ulcers on your legs from walking those swamps never seem to heal. Therefore, Mother, we have decided to retire you. You can continue going around to churches to raise support for the work, and we will send it out to Maude. But we will not agree to sending you back to Kelton again."

Dazed and feeling betrayed Eliza agreed to retire from the Convention, though in her heart she had no intention of retiring from Africa. For the next six years she traveled from church to church, from friend to friend, sharing her passion for the tribal people of Liberia. Many a night she spent in prayer, prevailing for the "children" she'd left behind and for the desperate needs of the tribal people in the interior of Liberia who had never heard about Jesus' love. After she'd formed several small Eliza Davis George Clubs to back her, Eliza felt the time had come to return to Africa to start over once more at seventy-two years of age.

A New Beginning

Eliza found herself dedicating a piece of ground, considered cursed by the natives to become her "life's work." She called it the Elizabeth Native Interior Mission—ENI. Once again Eliza built a mission out of the jungle. Growing rice and cassavas immediately became essential, so she worked out in the burning sun, bending from her waist down to "scratch rice" like every other Liberian countrywoman.

Painful ulcers on her leg, sometimes as deep as her bone, didn't keep her from hobbling along the trails to visit villages farther and farther in the jungle.

Otheliah, a young woman who helped care for Eliza, once made a list of Eliza's personal possessions, which included two or three dresses, a pair of sandals, a pair of high rubber boots, a single bed with two sheets, one blanket, and one pillow, a Bible, writing materials, and a sun helmet.

Eliza never seemed to have any use for money for herself. One of her "boys" explained it this way: "She used to spend money as if she didn't need it. She would tell us, 'Let's pray; the mission is out of money,' but when the money would come in you would see the people pour in to her saying, 'Mother, I don't have this or I need that.' On payday she would be completely broke; then we would go into another prayer meeting until finally somebody would provide."

While caring for dozens of children at the school she wanted to take a boy to the U.S. for training so that he could return to lead the work. Sadly, neither of the girls she'd pinned hopes on had fulfilled her dreams. Maude died within two years of returning to Africa, and Cerella married and left the ministry, so this time Eliza determined to take a boy.

She chose Augustus Marwieh, or Gus, as everyone called him. He had come to one of Mother's schools out of a remote jungle village without a stitch of clothing to his name, and he became one of her most promising students who evidenced great leadership potential.

Dreams Come True

Over the next twenty years Eliza traveled back and forth from ENI to the U.S., raising funds, and supervising ENI until

Gus finally took over. By the time of her death ENI mission had five primary schools, one high school, one technical school, and one hundred churches in the Independent Churches of Africa.

On one of her last trips to Liberia at age ninety-two, Gus took Mother Eliza far into the interior where the Gbaizon tribal church had invited her. Even on that trip Eliza would have preferred to walk, but porters carried her in a hammock through twenty-six swamps and eighteen streams on the three-day journey. At one point she had to make her way across a wide river where a big tree had been felled to span the distance. The porters could not balance the hammock across the log, so Eliza sat astride the "bridge" and worked her way across herself.

Eliza spoke at the final meeting with hundreds of Gbaizon people gathered. "Africa gave birth to black people. . . . I'm not ashamed of being black. My mother said to me, 'Liza, if I was a black man, I would go back to Africa.' When I was in my mother's womb, she said she had a longing to come to Africa; it came out in me. I love Africa; if I had a thousand lives, I'd give them all to God for Africa."

Eliza continued to share the passion of her heart wherever she went, even in the nursing home in Texas where she spent her last year. She died on March 9, 1979, at one hundred full years of age.

If you could ask Eliza Davis George what caused her to "finish well" perhaps she would have responded—

Live out your passion. Her passion to share the love of Christ with those who had never had the opportunity to hear of him was a high priority to her dying day.

Be a risk-taker. Her strong faith in God's ability to meet her needs enabled her to start out on journeys for which she had no funds; begin buildings for which she had no materials; take into the school children for whom she had no food. She trusted God to meet her needs as long as they were within the realm of his will.

Pray about everything. When Eliza challenged others to pray it was not an idle cliché. She believed in two basic solutions to all her problems and had followed this simple plan all her life: every situation and every need was immediately taken to her heavenly Father in prayer. While other people slept, Eliza prayed; when crises called for quick decisions, Eliza prayed; and when things got tougher than usual, she fasted.

Don't quit until you can't go on. Eliza did not let her physical limitations keep her from doing what God had called her to do. A friend reported that at ninety-nine years of age he heard Mother Eliza speak at a meeting. She threw her cane across the stage as if to say, "See, if I can still do it, you can." God gave her a resilient body and a determined mind, and she kept on going until she broke her hip and couldn't go anymore.

THREE

GROWING OLD IN THE TWENTY-FIRST CENTURY

We do not stop playing because we grow old; we grow old because we stop playing.

Mikey's Funnies
www.youthspecialties.com

The first time I traveled to Korea to meet with Christian women leaders, I felt embarrassed when they asked me, "How old are you?"

Startled at their seemingly audacious question I murmured, "Sixty-six."

Their dark eyes lit up and their faces broke into broad grins. Their curiosity urged them on. "How many children do you have?"

I felt more comfortable with this one and responded, "Five—four boys and one girl."

Now they clapped their hands in approval, and when they heard that I had eighteen grandchildren that seemed to be the crown jewel as they nodded knowingly to each other. I learned that age commands respect and honor in that Asian culture.

Age has probably never been so revered in the West. But anthropologist Ashley Montague recalls, "Until some time after World War II in Britain and Western Europe as well as in the United States, to be old was revered. Governments were run by graybeards, the world's business was conducted by old men and families were subject to the wills of their oldest members.

"Women, of course, suffered under this regime even more than men, because daughters were considered even more immature, more vulnerable, and more dependent than sons, and in greater need of supervision and protection."[1]

Much has changed since the turn of the twentieth century when the average life expectancy was a little over forty-seven years. By the year 2000 life expectancy for women had increased to eighty and continues to rise.

Bob Buford in his book *Game Plan* claims that actuarial statistics confirm this startling statement: "Most people who are fifty will live another thirty years. . . . A woman who is fifty, if she doesn't die of cancer or heart disease, will live to see her ninety-second birthday! Men are only slightly behind in this statistic."[2]

More than thirty-five million Americans have passed their sixty-fifth birthday—that's 12.4 percent of the population. This percentage will increase to 20 percent by 2030.[3] Women over eighty-five make up the fastest growing group in the United States and the world. Women must face the challenge of successful aging with courage and intentionality.

We would like "to live young while growing older and to die young as late as possible."[4] The writer of Psalms adds the dimension we all should seek: "Now that I am old and gray, don't forsake me. Give me time to tell this new generation (and their children too) about all your mighty miracles" (Psalm 71:18 TLB).

As women realize that they have been given a "thirty-year bonus," many wonder what they are going to do with the rest of their lives. We still live in a youth-oriented society as we noted in the last chapter. Older women, especially, experience a decline in opportunities and an increasing sense of a diminishing self. Yet the women I've met in the course of my research have helped to shatter some prevalent myths of aging we've come to accept.

Myth # 1: Physical Ailments Are Obstacles to a Purposeful Life

I can still see the sparkle in the eyes of eighty-two-year-old June, now bent over with osteoporosis, telling us about the "girl with the purple hair" she met on a bus and for whom she is praying and hoping to witness to.

I was amazed at seventy-eight-year-old Ione's capacity to enjoy life from her wheelchair and stay on top of issues in the society and the church, even while she cares for her husband who has Parkinson's disease.

My interview with Evelyn Christenson impressed me; I was amazed at the energy that propels this eighty-one-year-old best-selling author and speaker in spite of congestive heart failure, which reduces her heart's capacity to pump blood by 70 percent.

Health problems for the aging are no myth—few of us reach senior status without some kind of physical limitation. Forty-nine percent of noninstitutionalized elderly suffer from some form of arthritis; 36 percent have hypertension; and another 27 percent experience some kind of heart condition. However, the same study showed that three quarters of older Americans assessed their health as good.[5]

Responses to the questionnaire I sent out to Christian women on a mission organization's mailing list verified these findings. Seventy-seven percent of the women between the ages of fifty and ninety reported that they had good or excellent health.

While physical problems can pose a major concern as we grow older, most women continue to enjoy good enough health to stay active and interested in life into their "old-old" years. The vast majority of women will remain independent well into their eighties. Only 4.5 percent of persons sixty-five years and over live in nursing homes.[6] As we shall discover, attitude and trust in God's sovereignty enables many women to have a meaningful and fruitful old age, even in the face of physical limitations.

Myth # 2: Our Brain's Capacity Is on the Decline

As we age we may not consciously admit it but the fear of dementia lurks in the back of our minds like a fluttering moth. Unfortunately one person in four over age eighty is afflicted with Alzheimer's disease, and the rate increases with age. But in spite of that sobering statistic, for most of us, our aging brain does not decline as the years go by. More than 85 percent of the women who responded to my questionnaire indicated that compared to their early adulthood they considered their mental abilities to be every bit as good. I'm impressed by the acumen of the women with whom I talked about aging.

When I stayed in eighty-three-year-old Alvera Michelson's home, I listened with awe as she patiently taught a teenage Chinese immigrant how to play the violin. A widow for more than ten years, Alvera had written and edited theological textbooks with her husband before his death. She now edits articles for a Christian publication, teaches a Bible class, and volunteers at a local Christian organization.

Contrary to what most of us have heard, studies show that older people perform intellectually at much the same level as young adults. Of course changes occur in that the older minds usually operate slower, and short-term memory may decrease.

Lydia Bronte writes, "Most measurable aspects of intelligence and memory remain virtually unchanged well into the seventies and eighties as long as people remain healthy."[7]

We all forget names, appointments, where we left our keys. (It's not a sign of Alzheimer's to forget where you parked the car, but it may be if you forget you have a car.) Our brains have inventoried so much information over the decades that they operate on LIFO—last in, first out. Worrying about memory loss only exacerbates the problem. There are other causes for memory loss besides dementia, such as certain medications (for example, ranitidine for heartburn can temporarily affect memory for some), anxiety, depression, being overtired, or just having too many things going on at the same time.

We can help keep our aging brain cells from shrinking by living an active life, studying, reading, and doing crossword puzzles. Exercise, even in limited amounts, helps to keep our brains in shape. Perhaps one reason so many of the responders to my questionnaire felt comfortable with their mental condition (almost 100 percent of those who had earned an M.A. or Ph.D. degree felt that way) is that they keep up with conditions and needs in the Third World through their interest in missions, and they are vitally aware of news events that affect those interests. Involvement in God's worldwide program can stimulate thought at any age!

As we age, the advantages of accumulated experience and multiplicity of tests and triumphs we've gone through should enable us to deal with the challenges of life with wisdom. The information society of the twenty-first century depends on technology rather than the knowledge of the past and mental accumulation of facts. Little wonder older people find it more difficult to utilize their most valuable resource—wisdom and experience.

Richard Restak, a neurologist, wrote, "If you're looking for an area where we hold a clear advantage over youngsters, we've got one; the ability to put things in context and reach a good decision with less information—otherwise known as wisdom."[8] Restak points out that 40 percent of the nation's more than twelve hundred federal judges are over sixty-five.

The Old Testament refers to several "wise women" who were called upon to rectify difficult situations. We've already mentioned Deborah's long years of leadership in Israel. David averted a tragedy by following the wise advice of Abigail, who made up for her husband Nabal's pigheadedness by providing food for David's men (1 Sam. 25). Joab, a leader of David's cabinet, sought the help of the "wise woman of Tekoa" to speak to David when he refused to be reconciled with his son Absalom. In response to her counsel, David recalled his son to Jerusalem (2 Sam. 14:1–23).

Someone has suggested that we would benefit from councils of "wise" men and women who could deal with large-scale problems of life, life planning, and correcting mistakes. But opportunities for wise elders to utilize their gifts of wisdom are often limited in our society.

Myth # 3: Creativity Decreases with Age

Energy and even ambition may decrease with age, but people can be just as creative in their senior years as in their youth. Michelangelo did his best work after eighty; Edison continued to invent at eighty-two; Monet painted the *Water Lily Pond* at seventy-six; Benjamin Franklin invented bifocals at seventy-eight.

Grandma Moses defied the myth. Having lived on a farm all her life she realized at seventy-five that she was too old to farm and too young to sit on the porch in a rocking chair. She produced her highly acclaimed paintings until she died at 101.

Some of us are just late starters. Perhaps the creative juices needed time to "cook" or we didn't have time earlier to learn to paint, to write, to start a new organization.

Creativity demands a certain amount of risk-taking. I was sixty-two when Luis Bush, executive director of the AD2000 & Beyond Movement, asked me to start a global women's network. I had no idea where to begin or how to work with women from many cultures. But over the next ten years I had the time of my life mobilizing and encouraging women to use their gifts to reach out in evangelism and prayer. Meeting extraordinary women around the world inspired me to write *Women as Risk-Takers for God* [9] in my seventieth year.

For some, creativity grows over the years. Newly married, Jan and her husband couldn't afford to purchase Christmas gifts for their family, so they improvised by using their artistic abilities to create character dolls. Their first dolls, designed in 1952, were a set of carolers and a family of peasants.

More than fifty years later they sell Simpich Character Dolls all over the world. Their shop is a storybook land of Dickens figures, nativity characters, pilgrims, elves, and fairies, which stand twelve to fourteen inches tall and are dressed in authentic costumes detailed to the tiniest button and delicate lace collar. Jan continues to shape the women's intricate faces, working the super-sculpy, a type of clay, until the eyes reflect the doll's character and the mouth breaks into just the right expression. Sometimes this process takes weeks and many trials, but she knows when she's gotten her latest creation just right.

In the second half of life, we may be challenged to recognize our creative talents and to find ways to release them. Unfortunately our culture has encouraged us to internalize our limitations, and we settle for less than using the God-given gifts hidden in our hearts. Finding our creative springs may take intentionality—making time and place to release them into the open.

At seventy-three Stan Freberg, satirist and composer, muses on his creative abilities, "In my creative life I haven't had too many lows. I never worry about my talent because that comes from the Lord anyhow. Reading gets my creative juices going. I also get ideas while I drive or when I'm in the shower."[10] (I find mine in the bathtub!)

The Difficult Realities of Aging

Not everything about the stress and pain of aging is a myth. We do get physically weaker; we do enter nursing homes (4.5 percent of people over sixty-five in the U.S.); we do succumb to Alzheimer's (25 percent over age eighty); we do face death (100 percent).

Uncertainties cloud our financial future. While most of the women who responded to my questionnaire described their financial situation as good or excellent, at least 30 percent said "poor or fair."

Consider Sue, who has been divorced for a number of years. Several years ago she started a small business but couldn't make it go, and she lost all her savings. At sixty-four she realizes that she will have to continue to work for years to come. She says she is downsizing and sorting through her belongings to simplify her life.

On the other hand when seventy-year-old Lois was asked what she finds best about this stage in life she responded, "The freedom to pick and choose my activities; to have the financial ability to travel as we wish and to go on Elderhostel trips." Lois and her husband maintain a winter home in Arizona while spending summers in Michigan. They represent the 14 percent of family households over sixty-five with an income of more than $75,000 a year.

Sue is fortunate in that she has a college degree and marketable skills. Education not only affects income but also our sense of physical attractiveness and self-image. In 2000 only 16 percent of the U.S. population over sixty-five had a college degree. Most older women have to settle for jobs in lower paying sales and service jobs. More than a quarter of the women between sixty-five and seventy-nine who responded to the questionnaire said they were still working full- or part-time. Even with women's increasing earning ability in the United States, those over sixty-five still earn 44 percent less than older men. Widows living only on social security fall well below the poverty line, and those older than sixty-five are twice as likely to be poor as men of that age. Fortunately as the younger baby boomers reach senior status, they bring with them higher education and career skills, which should improve this picture.

Eventually most of us will deal with some kind of retirement; this comes in different forms for women. Busy mothers face empty nests; wives face widowhood; career women lose their positions. In some ways retirement may be easier for women than for men. Women are generally more relational, more involved in social activities and intimate friendships, and find it easier to maintain a rich life after their primary career is over.

With planning and intentionality, this new phase of life can be the most wonderful time of all. Now we reap the harvest of years of experience, walking with God, applying his Word, and obeying his will. We'll discuss retirement more fully in chapter 5.

Kathleen Fischer in *Autumn Gospel* poignantly compares this season of life to autumn. "The days are gorgeous and full of color, but I know that it will be cold at night and get dark earlier. It is a very good time, but more lies behind than ahead."[11]

This awareness may lead to depression. Clinical depression generally begins in youth or young adulthood and may be genetic. While 21 percent of all women suffer from depression at some time in their lives, depression is not necessarily a part of aging. But the losses, loneliness, and chronic illness that often come with aging can result in depression. A great deal can be done to cure depression today, both medically and psychologically. Prayer and the love and support of the body of Christ can play a major role in finding healing.

I didn't know that my mother was depressed until we came home from Africa in 1977. In her earlier years she had been cheerful and optimistic in spite of her difficult life. After my alcoholic father died of cirrhosis of the liver, she courageously rose from years of caring for him at home and took a job as dorm mother at a Christian college.

But an insidious blood condition weakened her so that she gave up working. She lived on the princely sum of $276 from social security and her quarterly AT&T dividends from a small number of stocks my father had received from his company. I don't know how many trips she took alone to the doctor to get a blood transfusion, which would energize her for a while again.

After we moved to California I depended on phone calls back to the Midwest to keep in touch, but communication was difficult. Hearing my mother's leaden voice, the toneless responses, and the lack of interest in any topic I tried to raise was painful for me. Getting her to talk was like squeezing toothpaste out of an empty tube.

It became obvious that my mother could not stay alone in her senior apartment, especially in the cold Wisconsin winters. I pictured her shuffling out on the slippery sidewalk to clear the snow off her car and worried about her driving on icy roads. Since she found it almost impossible to make a decision my brother and I made it for her and moved her to California.

I saw for myself what clinical depression could do. She wept when she saw her tiny new apartment; she cried herself to sleep when she realized she had no car and would never drive again; she sat in her lounge chair staring out the window hour after hour like a prisoner on death row. When she went to a Christian psychologist he told her to write ten things she could do for others each day—that her happiness was her choice. Sadly she never found her way up and out of the heaviness, and she died in the grip of depression in 1982.

How different it would have been twenty years later, in spite of her pre-leukemia, her limited finances, and her lonely life. Medical treatment is available today, and we should not allow a perceived stigma to keep us from seeking it for ourselves or for friends and loved ones entrapped by depression.

So, what is it like to grow old in the twenty-first century? We can find a life of fulfillment, meaning, and purpose in spite of the concurrent accoutrements of aging. We may be full of physical energy and enjoy independent living well past eighty-five. Or we may face a time of adjusting to the loss of our dearest companion in life or of physical strength. Pain and dependency may be our lot.

Whatever condition God allows us to finish with, he expects us to finish well, confident in his care, rejoicing in his faithfulness and determined to make every moment count until we take our last breath. From her wheelchair, our next model of finishing well demonstrates the positive attitude it takes to do just that.

Some of us are just beginning to think about aging or perhaps feel it's too soon to do that. But if you're reading this, and God spares you from accident or terminal illness, you *are* going to age in the twenty-first century! Are you looking forward to the rest of your life?

Ione Larson

ATTITUDE IS A DECISION

Life seems to have given Ione Larson more jolts than one person can handle—from paralysis to her husband's Parkinson's disease. But she has risen to the occasion like cream in an old-fashioned milk bottle. Her attitude makes the difference!

Whenever I think of Ione Larson I can see her sliding from her wheelchair into the front seat of her car. With several deft moves she folds up her wheelchair, lifts it into the backseat, and pulls her body over to the driver's side. I can hear her clear, soft voice saying, "I'll just *run* down to the church to pick up some books."

In 1951 Ione had indeed been running. At twenty-six she was caring for her husband, a two-year-old son, a six-month-old daughter, and visiting her mother who was dying of cancer. But one day three weeks after her mother's death she started having a fever, and her body ached all over. Thinking it was flu she took aspirin and tried to carry on at home, but her head began to ache violently, and her neck became stiff and sore. By the time her husband Don came home from work she was having spasms throughout her body.

"I felt as though something very heavy was stomping on me," she remembers.

Don called their family doctor, who came right over to the house. The doctor seemed to take a long time examining her, and Ione grew apprehensive.

"I think it's appendicitis," she remarked faintly. "It hurts right here," pointing to her side.

The doctor responded, "Let's hope it is."

He obviously suspected something far more serious, for he told Don that he would have to do a spinal tap to make sure of his diagnosis.

The two men lifted Ione onto the dining room table, and Don held her hands, dripping sweat from every pore of his body, while the doctor performed the painful procedure.

A Life-Changing Diagnosis

That afternoon the doctor called to confirm their worst suspicions: polio. He ordered her to the county hospital immediately, since the disease had reached a highly contagious stage. While Don's mother stayed with the children, now exposed as well, he drove Ione to the isolation ward at the hospital where everyone with the dreaded disease was taken. Ione remembers that many other young mothers as well as children shared the ward with her. Thankfully her own two children escaped the crippling disease.

"I could have walked in that afternoon," Ione recalls. "But by the next morning I was paralyzed to my knees; the next day to my hips; and then to my chin with the exception of my arms. I had more pain than anyone else. The spasms lasted for thirty days."

In the fifties doctors could not do a great deal for polio patients. Ione remembers the smelly warm blankets and her reaction to heavy doses of codeine to control the pain. When she left the hospital two-and-a-half months later (to the tune of $500) she was told that she would never walk again. How does a mother care for a two-year-old and an infant in that condition?

For three years Ione used a wheelchair, but with therapy and grit she learned to get on her feet using braces and crutches and even to drive her car.

For the next twenty-five years Ione managed to "walk" with leg braces and a cane. With his typical ingenuity, Don had made a tripod over her bed so she could lift herself out. Ione grins when she says that it later became a swing for the children when she didn't need it anymore. Only when the strain on her knees became too much and arthritis added to her problems did she finally give in to a wheelchair in her mid-fifties. Now she could wheel around, which actually gave her more freedom and enabled her to carry things on her lap.

Ione focused on prayer and faith as key factors in bringing her through her illness. She explains, "When I had polio the Lord healed me right away of resentment and anger, and he helped me to understand that I was a real person in his sight. I was still I, even though I was handicapped from polio. I had so much to live for—the children, my husband, a new house. We had such wonderful prospects, not only materially but also spiritually. I was determined not to miss out on that."

Preparation for Difficult Times

Ione's background seemed to have prepared her to weather tough storms in life. Her father had left the family when her mother was pregnant with their fifth child. His parting words to Ione were, "You take care of your mother and brothers and sisters. I'm leaving you in charge until I come back." He never came back.

The family moved to Santa Cruz on Grandma Pinckard's farm. Both Ione's mother and grandmother had a college-education, a rarity in those days. Though the depression took its toll, Grandmother Pinckard got a job as a technical nurse in San Francisco, earning $50 a month to help support her daughter and five grandchildren.

"To this day I hate seersucker or striped dresses," Ione confesses. Women earned a little money sewing dresses for the WPA (Work Projects Administration, a government program to help the jobless). They gave these dresses, which all looked alike, to people on welfare. Ione also remembers standing in line with her brother waiting for free government sacks of beans and flour while her mother and the other children stood in another line for cheese and lard. To add to the farm's meager income, her mother took in washing and did dressmaking. Later she started cleaning houses for people.

"We always gave a tithe to the church, but Mother had us save our money as much as possible for college," Ione recalls. "Even though we were very poor, we were brought up to be the best we could. My mother was terribly strict. The teachers even remarked, 'You McFarlanes are the best-mannered children in the whole school.'"

Ione met Don while she was working her way through San Jose State College to earn a degree in education. One summer she worked in the cannery in Santa Cruz. "My job was to run my hands through the peach and apricot waste going past on a belt to make sure there were no sticks or stones to break up the equipment."

Ione met many servicemen engaged in the war in the Pacific who helped at the cannery. She says, "I learned to say 'no' in five languages."

One Sunday evening after church a young naval officer came up to her and said, "Wait here until I find somebody to introduce us." Two weeks later Don Larson asked her to marry him.

Don was from a very different background and had grown up in the mountains and forests of Oregon. He and his brother fished and hunted together, and very early he began working with his father, manufacturing logging tools. Eventually he developed that skill into a successful tool business in San Jose. Ione found him considerate, thoughtful, and interesting to talk to. "But most of all he was a stable person," she explains. "I realized I wanted somebody on whom I could depend."

A Fruitful Life despite Limitations

Indeed, Don proved his dependability, especially after Ione returned home from the hospital partially paralyzed. He creatively designed ways to make it easier for her to get around the house, building ramps and putting up rails. In spite of his heavy work designing and producing logging tools, he always had time to do the grocery shopping and take other responsibilities off Ione's shoulders.

Ione herself determined to be and do everything God wanted for her. She became active in the local Presbyterian church, serving as an elder and being involved in various committees. One day a friend asked if she was ever going to do anything outside the "golden ghetto."

In response to this challenge she joined the League of Women Voters and eventually became president of the local chapter.

When her term was over her successor asked if she would do a TV program sponsored by the League, called *Up Front and Center.* Ione had never even been in a TV studio before, but she soon learned to anchor the program with grace and charm. She loved doing the research before interviewing the political figures who appeared on the program.

She especially remembers interviewing Ronald Reagan, whom she describes as "perfectly charming, a delightful person to talk to," even though he complained about the League's lack of support for one of his propositions. Ione hosted the weekly half-hour show for almost ten years.

Through her TV contacts she became aware of the work of the San Jose Food Bank, which she considered one of the best-run nonprofits in the Bay Area. Her interest soon led to deeper involvement, and she became president of the board, serving in that capacity for five years.

In a wheelchair by this time, Ione nevertheless took a trip to Mexico City representing her church's mission involvement with Latin America Mission. Nothing stopped her. She even visited the villages on the garbage dump.

This was not her first interest in international missions. She and Don had been involved as volunteers with Partners International, a mission that supports national ministries rather than western missionaries. Because of Ione's involvement in communications, President Allen Finley asked her to help produce slide presentations for the national leaders who came to the U.S. to present their ministries.

This began a ten-year ministry with Partners International. One of the highlights was her visit to Brazil in 1987 for a continent-wide mission conference which many of the global leaders of Partners attended. It took a lot of courage for her to travel to a city like Sao Paulo, knowing there would be few accommodations that had handicap access.

When some of Partners' national leaders arranged a visit to a mission outside of Sao Paulo, Ione demurred, realizing that not only would there be difficult terrain to maneuver with her wheelchair, but that the bus would be inaccessible.

Many of these ministry leaders who came from places like Nairobi, Hong Kong, and Delhi, had been the objects of Ione's loving and meticulous care of them when they had been in the States. They wouldn't hear of leaving her behind. Instead they lifted the wheelchair into the bus and over the rough trails and made sure that she saw every corner of Antioch Mission that they saw.

Retirement Brings Changes

Ione and Don had always enjoyed sharing their diverse work experiences. She found Don extremely supportive and encouraging as she ventured into new programs. When the time came for Don to retire, Ione decided to quit her job so they could travel and share new experiences together.

They linked up with organizations of wheelchair travelers to visit Great Britain and take a Caribbean cruise. Even with the best of care wheelchair traveling can prove hazardous. On one flight the attendants dropped Ione as they were helping her to the bathroom, and she suffered a broken leg, which involved a hospital stay in London. Ione recalls, "It was all free—the British taxpayers paid for it."

A few years later Ione took another fall—this time out of the wheelchair when her wheels caught in poorly repaired flooring at the grocery store. This time she sprained her left leg.

Ione admits, "I resented it very much. It was a time that we could still have traveled together." The fall ended the Larsons' travel, but the insurance settlement paid for a new van with a wheelchair lift. At seventy-five Ione learned to drive with hand controls. (Even she concedes it was getting unsafe for her to use her paralyzed right leg on the brake by pushing it down with her hand!) She proudly points out all the gadgets, which she can manipulate at the touch of a button.

In the early nineties Don began complaining of flulike symptoms. He felt very tired and ached all over, and when the symptoms didn't disappear he visited their doctor, who sent Don to a neurologist. The diagnosis shattered Don and Ione. Parkinson's disease.

With her usual cheerful attitude toward life, Ione took Don's illness in stride. Though Don felt tired and often depressed, the medicines kept the worst symptoms at bay. Ione recalls, "For the first five years or so we lived a fairly normal life."

From Care Receiver to Caregiver

Don grew steadily worse. Though his tremors are under control, he freezes frequently, and Ione has to be right there to remind him to take one step at a time. His mental deterioration causes the greatest difficulty. Because the brain is not able to make the connections from one synapse to the other, he usually can only think of the first step of a process. He can't make his mind leap to the next step. He becomes very frustrated, and Ione often tries to help him step-by-step through a project he's working on.

Don maintains a tool shop in the garage, surrounding himself with choice pieces of equipment from his business. Ione was concerned that since many of the electrical tools use 220 volts he could electrocute himself, and she finally stopped him from using them.

Many times a day she rolls her wheelchair down the ramp Don built into the garage to call out, "Don, are you all right?" Sometimes she finds drawers of screws, wires, and small tools scattered all over the floor with Don just looking bewildered as he tries to find something. Patiently she'll ask him what he's looking for and tries to help him find it.

One morning Don woke her up at four o'clock with a glass in his hand.

"Look, Ione. I've made Sangria," he proudly exclaimed.

Not too thrilled about hauling herself out of bed into her wheelchair at this hour of the morning, Ione asked sleepily, "Where did you find the wine and orange juice to make it?"

"I found the wine on the top shelf in the bedroom closet," Don replied, sounding pleased with himself. "I couldn't find any orange juice, but I found a bottle of orange powder in the kitchen. Here, taste it. It's great. I'm on my second glass."

To please him, Ione took a sip. "It's pretty good, Don." To herself she added, "But you've used that expensive bottle of wine I was saving for a special occasion."

And then she realized the "orange powder" was Metamucil. Now wide-awake she told Don what he'd done, and they both laughed until the tears flowed.

When Ione tells this story she ends it with a flourish: "Light the candles and put on soft music; can you think of a more elegant or romantic way to take a laxative?"

Ione has found that maintaining her ability to laugh helps her keep things in perspective. In these later years this many-talented woman finds that her major responsibility focuses on caring for her life's companion. Neither her father's desertion nor her debilitating illness constrained her life as much as this latest blow.

"Sometimes I feel as though I've been put on a shelf," she confesses. "The inside of me gets very rebellious. But I'm also blessed because the person who I was before could never have been able to deal with some of the things with Don—which he can't help. He leaves things all over, and I have to watch him all the time. Once he began cutting down the neighbors' hedge. I had to rush out to stop him."

She pauses to organize her thoughts. "I wasn't prepared to take care of someone who needed constant watching over—to having to listen for someone all the time—to get up in the night when he's hallucinating. Don and I still have conversations but not as much as we used to. I've become more like a mother or a teacher. I hate having to remind him all the time to do this and that."

Inner Strength

Ione seldom allows feelings of depression to take over; instead she still dreams. "We want to stay in this house as long as we can. I finally found a cleaning service that does more than the middle of the room.

"There are so many resources for caregivers. My children are wonderful. Sarah, our granddaughter, walks with Don every week. She's an architect, so she helps me a lot with things like broken pipes in the yard.

"The church is immeasurably wonderful. I can call the deacons anytime. And the geriatric team of the Veterans Administration has been a great help with things we need around the house."

But more than the outside resources is Ione's inner strength—her spiritual core—her faith and trust in her Lord. She works hard at maintaining her mental abilities and tries to read at least three books a week. She keeps up with world events inspired by her hands-on experience with missions. She uses her computer to keep in touch with friends or to search the Web.

Though she doesn't like to drive at night anymore, she opens her home to others. When she's asked to serve on a committee at church she says, "Sure, as long as you can come to my house."

Interaction with people helps her maintain her sense of dignity and self-worth. When the local woman pastor started a group study of Henri Nouwen's book *Turn My Mourning into Dancing,* Ione invited them to her home. "Twelve women came to my house every Wednesday night. It was delightful."

What advice does she give to other caregivers? "Don't get trapped into thinking you're the only one who can take care of your care receiver. Twice a week she takes Don to a day-care center for seniors, which he enjoys and which gives her some private downtime.

"There are many resources," Ione adds. "Try to get away even in your own mind. It's important to be with other people and to have a spiritual core."

The positive attitudes Ione practiced when she suffered the ravages of polio at twenty-six have stood her in good stead as she faces the test of her strength and dignity while nearing her ninth decade.

"How do I want to finish my life?" she asks. "Like my grandmother who lived to ninety-eight, sharp as a tack and praising the Lord every day. I would like to be the kind of example that shows the love of Christ and can express that love to my family and in the community."

Even now she dreams about working on a project at the church providing affordable housing for the *less fortunate.* And those words are totally defined by her attitude!

FOUR

HOW BABY BOOMERS CAN PREPARE FOR THE SECOND HALF OF LIFE

"... to be made new in the attitude of your minds."

Ephesians 4:23

Be what you are ...

Os Guinness

World War II spawned the highest birthrate in this country's history. More than seventy-six million babies were born between 1946 and 1964, the eighteen years following the end of the war. The first of these baby boomers turned fifty in 1996.

The boomer cohort moved through society like a "pig in a python," inflating sales of baby foods, expanding schools, increasing college enrollments—and is threatening to overwhelm the social security system. Sixty percent of baby boomers polled do not believe that social security will have enough funding for their retirement.

In the sixties and seventies the pig in the python reached its teens and twenties. It was the "age of rebellion." Headlines blared about anger with the Vietnam War, drug experimentation, calls for legalizing pot, hippies and flower children, the revolution in sex and music.

New Expectations

While parents and grandparents shook their heads in dismay, boomers became the high-tech workforce of the nineties, enjoying an immediate prosperity their elders had taken long years to achieve. With added years and improved health care, boomers anticipate the challenges of aging in a different way than their grandparents did.

In her landmark book *New Passages* Gail Sheehy wrote, "When our parents turned fifty, we thought they were old. They thought they were old. Society told them they were old and they acted old. But today, women and men I have interviewed for *New Passages* routinely believe they are five to ten years younger than the age on their birth certificate. . . . Fifty is now what 40 used to be."[1]

Sheehy found that most women in their fifties felt more fulfilled and enjoyed greater well-being than at any other stage in their lives. These physically young and active women will probably live well into their eighties and even nineties. A fifty-year-old woman could well have a whole additional life ahead of her.

The baby boomers will likely see age as an adventure. They sense that something new will happen as they age. Consider these responses from women who answered this query in a Denver newspaper: "Are you . . . over 50 and fabulous?"

I've rejected the notion that age is a barrier and once my "nest" was empty, I felt eager to experience and accomplish new things. Tammy, 56

One of the things that help me feel young is my involvement with young people. I love working with the youth in my church. Betty, 50-plus

I work out, I eat correctly with the help of a nutritionist. I don't smoke or drink. I have a spiritual program and am available for attitude adjustments when needed. Boring? Dull? Not to me. I have never had more energy, vitality, curiosity or passion for life. This is, by far, the best time ever. Susan, 50-plus

I did not have patience at 15. I did not have perspective at 20. I did not have understanding at 30; I did not have wisdom at 40. Fifty is fabulous! Joann, 55

My positive outlook on life keeps me both physically and spiritually healthy, as well as energetic. I am just now starting to peak because I cherish my job, my family and my friends. Life is good! Judi, 55[2]

When Change Is Needed

Not all women hold positive attitudes about their lives as they grow older. Many are treading water in dead-end jobs they simply tolerate; others struggle with restrictions and negative attitudes in their marriages; some are overcome with a shrinking self-image, especially as they see gray hair and wrinkles when they look in the mirror. They struggle with a sense of hopelessness rather than optimism, dreading what could become a long and less useful existence.

No wonder psychologist and pastor Dallas Shafer warns, "If you're thirty-five and you're not planning for this dimension [the possibility of longevity] you are losing vital time in preparing for where God can take you in a whole new and different role."[3]

Shafer foresees the tragedy of women unprepared for the challenges of empty nest, possible divorce, or widowhood. He stresses the importance of couples sitting down together to talk about the next phase of life and especially how the wife can move on to develop and use her gifts.

He is rightly concerned about abuse in the Christian home but adds a troubling dimension, "The one area of abuse which is totally neglected is the over-controlling man. Finally the kids are gone. Talk about a woman on the horns of dilemma. She's been put down for twenty-five years while raising the kids, had to beg for money to buy groceries while he drives a big pickup. Here you have a very bright, beaten-down woman. You get her away from her husband and she lights up like a Christmas tree. But he won't let her move on. He stands on biblical principle that 'you're to be in submission to me.'"

Planning to make the longer span of life ahead meaningful for married couples must begin with open communication and seeking God's direction together. A confident, self-assured husband will allow his wife the freedom to develop fully into the person God wants her to be. He may even take the initiative to encourage her, recognizing her hidden gifts and the sacrifice of personal development she has willingly made in order to be the mother their children needed.

Bob Buford calls this mid-period of life "half time"—time to sit down and evaluate where you are and where you want to go.

Failure at Half Time

Half times may take you by surprise during a wrenching disappointment. Take my husband and me for example. We had been missionaries in South Africa for twenty-two years, most of that time involved in an exciting youth ministry. We turned the program over to African leadership and were planning to open a Communications Center at the request of mission leadership. However, we ran into stiff resistance to the concept of coordinating the mission's communications ministries under one leader and down the road turning it over to African leadership. As resistance to change usually happens, it eventually focused on us personally.

Many evenings my husband and I prayed about what to do. We wanted to stay in Africa where we saw great needs and opportunities, but we felt we were fighting a losing battle. During that time riots and demonstrations increased as African youth resisted the ever-tightening noose of apartheid laws. Rioters burned schools and other buildings in Soweto, the township outside of Johannesburg. Our African coworkers warned us not to come out to the township, for our safety and theirs.

One night as we prayed God gave us a clear answer. It was time to go back to the United States. We had just received a publication from Wheaton Graduate School about its winter schedule. A new semester would open in three weeks. I had already taken courses for my master's degree, but I needed another semester on the Illinois campus. Always eager to help me develop my gifts, my husband suggested that we return to the States in time for me to enter graduate school. Four of our children already studied there and the fifth had completed high school, so we were free to make the change. "I'll even take care of the house while you study," my husband promised.

In a whirlwind three weeks we sold everything, packed our personal belongings, and settled into a furnished house in Wheaton, Illinois. I was forty-nine years old, and my life has never been the same.

I didn't have the baby boomers' attitude toward aging, and I confess I felt guilty and embarrassed about sitting in the classroom with bright young students. I wondered if the professors thought I was wasting their time—after all, what would I be able to accomplish in the limited time remaining?

God has since shown me that the course corrections initiated by failure prepared me for a totally unexpected stage in my life, filled with excitement and unimagined joy.

Planning Ahead

The Bible is the story of God's plans. Through eons before time, God's planning committee, the Persons of the Trinity, must have planned the creation in every detail of the universe right down to the hairs on our head. God planned the coming of the Messiah (Isa. 9:6), the messenger who would pave the way for him (Mal. 3:1). He prepared for his kingdom since the creation of the world (Matt. 25:34) and plans a place for us in eternity (John 14:2).

God's plans are always completed: "What I have said, that will I bring about; what I have planned, that will I do" (Isa. 46:11b).

Our plans often go awry because they don't merge with his. A few of the respondents to my questionnaire replied that they only make plans one day at a time. "I don't plan ahead," wrote one woman. "I'm available for God's leading." In fact, 13 percent of the women who returned the completed questionnaire did not even respond to the question, "What plans do you have to make the remaining years of your life meaningful and fulfilling? What are you doing now to prepare?"

But many indicated that they were partnering with God in his plans for them. This open-ended question elicited a wide variety of answers that give us some idea of the preparations and plans of the 159 women between the ages of fifty and sixty-four who responded. Most of these responses also emerged in the live focus groups I held, where free-flowing discussions stimulated more in-depth response.

Here are the ten top-ranking responses revealing what this group of women is doing to prepare for a meaningful longer life.

1. Intentionally developing sensitivity to God's leading; spiritual growth; prayer
2. Short-term mission trips
3. Bible study
4. Planning retirement finances, long-term care
5. Continuing education—secular, seminary, and special courses
6. Focusing on global issues, missions
7. Focusing on doing parachurch ministries
8. Church involvement; teaching Bible studies and Sunday school
9. Moving to a smaller home or retirement community; downsizing
10. Exercising and caring for my health; proper diet

Understandably women in their eighties and nineties may feel that their life's course has been set and that the road lies fairly straight ahead. But 65 percent of the women who responded were under sixty-five years old and will have opportunity to prepare to make major course changes if needed. With an extended life span comes the distinct possibility that we may face loss of job, divorce or widowhood, and physical disabilities. Most mothers will have empty nests by their early fifties. Are we ready?

We trust God to direct our lives and fulfill his plans for us. What a comfort to know that when the road ahead looks dark, our heavenly Father knows the way we should take. "No eye has seen, no ear has heard, no mind has conceived what God has prepared for those who love him—but God has revealed it to us by his Spirit" (1 Cor. 2:9–10a).

Does this lessen the responsibility to prepare as best we can for the future with the help of the Holy Spirit? I think not. Peter challenges us: "have your minds ready for action" (1 Peter 1:13 GNT). We need to prepare ourselves in whatever way we can so that we are ready for doors God might open to us—or those he might shut.

Timothy encourages us to be "useful to the Master and prepared to do any good work" (2 Tim. 2:21). It may be that we're doing exactly what God wants us to do at this stage in life. That need not keep us from dreaming about what else God may have for us, to be available for anything he wants to do with our life. We can ask ourselves, "What happened to the dream I had when I was younger? What are the goals I promised myself I would reach? In what direction is the Holy Spirit nudging me now?"

Steps to a New You

Or to put the question another way, "What has God wired me for?" Bob Buford, in his book *Game Plan,* challenges, "I don't believe God wires you for advertising and then directs you to social work."[4] God has not wired us all to home-school, to make our homes a center of hospitality, or to serve as an administrative assistant in an office. Many women have spent the first half of their lives focusing on things for which they are not necessarily wired, but out of a spirit of love and concern for the welfare of their children they have willingly played that role, either in or outside of the home. Now with a new freedom and the possibility of long years ahead it's time to prepare to put our dreams into motion.

Even while caring for home and children it is possible to prepare for the next stage of life, at the same time passing on to our children interests and challenges that enrich their growth. Elaine Partnow writes in *Breaking the Age Barrier*, "The most graceful and productive way for a mother to encourage independence in her offspring is to find some independence for herself just as soon as the demands of toddlerism will allow."[5]

Ruth Heil speaks in churches and women's groups all over Germany and writes a quarterly column for *Lydia* magazine, the largest Christian women's publication in German-speaking Europe. This mother of ten children decided early in her career as wife and mother that she needed to do something to improve herself. During her pregnancy before each of her children was born Ruth developed a new interest or skill. She started playing the flute before her oldest son, Markus, arrived. Later she learned to play the accordion, then the guitar, and then learned to type. She took up painting and crocheting and developed her speaking and writing skills, which opened doors for her all over Germany.

In their traditional wooden house in the village of Fishbach Ruth had her own get-away room. When the glass-paneled door was closed the children knew this was Mother's private time. Ruth explained that she felt happy in those times away from the hubbub of the household. "The danger is," she says, "that mothers feel like [their children's] servants. And that feeling is not good for your child or for yourself. . . . Teenagers sometimes ask, 'Why didn't you do anything? Why didn't you build yourself up?'"[6]

Now that her children are grown, this woman who prepared herself when she was young utilizes all these gifts she developed in the ministry to which God has called her.

Some of us are dissatisfied with what we are accomplishing or even who we are. We've reached a plateau and are in danger of getting stuck.

Phyllis, a woman in her late forties, has done just that. She majored in anthropology in college but could never figure out what to do with it. She worked for the county with unmarried mothers for a few years after her marriage, but once her own children arrived she was happy to stay at home as a full-time mom.

By the time their children had reached high school she and her husband decided that she should get a job to help prepare for the expenses of college. After months of searching she took a job as a manager of a small office. At first she felt challenged by the opportunities to learn new skills and to bring the organization to a new level of success. But after a few years the routine became boring and with no opportunity for advancement or change, she resigned. Unfortunately she had not been preparing for other options and did not know what to do next.

Phyllis had broken the first law of the jungle, which according to Bob Buford is: "Have another vine in sight before you release the one you have hold of."[7] This is exactly what JoAnn felt she must do.

A New Direction

JoAnn Brechbill lived in the breathtaking beauty of the Oregon forests with her two sons and loved her job with the Forest Service. It had taken a divorce to turn her life back to God and the church, and she soon found, in spite of the painful experience, acceptance and opportunities to serve. She became an elder in her church, and the pastor frequently asked her to preach when he couldn't be there. "I was terrified," she recalls, "but I did it."

As she drove to her appointments through the serene quietness of God's creation, she had lots of time to pray and to listen to God. She began to realize that her service in the church was far more vitalizing than the forestry job she loved. God was beginning to nudge out the latent gifts and passion that she had been unaware of. She tried to resist the call into ministry, feeling it was just a whim of her imagination. But as parishioners commended and encouraged her, the call grew more urgent.

She faced tremendous obstacles. "I was a woman, I was divorced, I was sole support of two children, I didn't have an undergraduate degree, and I lived hundreds of miles from a college." And she was fifty years old!

Yet, providentially she had opportunity to relocate to Portland where she was able to go to college while she worked. Later she moved to Berkeley, California, where she completed her degree at fifty-five. She retired from her job and entered Gordon-Conwell Seminary.

Today JoAnn serves as Minister of Congregational Care in a large church. She brings to her ministry the experiences of her painful divorce, the struggles of being a single parent, the business acumen she gained through years in secular work, an in-depth training in the Word of God, and a heart that has been fine-tuned to serve with compassion.

JoAnn will be the first to admit that a career change as drastic as hers is daunting, especially for a woman. "In my younger days I'd never seen a woman in ministry. It remained a problem for me until I went to Berkeley, where my pastor, Dr. Earl Palmer, gave me a biblical perspective for women in ministry. Then I realized it's not a problem in the Bible, but it may be in culture or society."[8]

How to Start Preparing for the Second Half

Whether you feel you're stuck on a plateau and going nowhere, or whether you feel fulfilled in what you're doing, as JoAnn was, it is not too soon to think about preparing for the inevitable changes ahead. Don't be afraid of the risk of breaking old patterns or taking time to dream of new possibilities. Some of us are simply late starters, but that does not mean we can't rise to as high a level of achievement as many who started earlier.

Above all we need to live intentionally to utilize the gifts God has given us, desiring to make this, our one and only life, the best that it can be to the very end.

For some the thought of adding even one more responsibility is depressing. The taxi-moms and the "sandwich" daughters are barely getting enough sleep to keep them awake on their jobs. This kind of pressure forced Ruth Heil to retreat behind her glass-paneled door for self-preservation in "little dreams" that kept adding to her sense of personal fulfillment.

Let's look more closely at some of the ways you can prepare for the possible long years ahead. No matter whether you're a baby boomer just beginning to think about your inevitable aging or already designated a "senior citizen" by our society, it's neither too early nor too late to take some of these steps.

"Keep in Step with the Spirit"

As I grow older I find that keeping in step with the Holy Spirit (Gal. 5:25b) is just as important as when I was making the life-changing decisions of my youth. Listening to God's direction is vital at every stage of life so we don't drag behind his leading or run ahead of his will. It goes without saying that personal time with God is the basis for keeping in step.

Beyond growing in intimacy with the Lord there are other ways you can keep in step. One is an internal assessment of where you are at this stage of life. It's time to look yourself straight in the eye and ask:

What are my strengths? What do I do best?
What are my weaknesses? Where have I failed and why?

> What are my natural abilities and talents? What affirmation have I received from others?
>
> What are my spiritual gifts? How could I use them better?

In his book *Your Spiritual Gifts Can Help Your Church Grow,* Peter Wagner defines a spiritual gift as "a special attribute given by the Holy Spirit to *every member* of the body of Christ, according to God's grace, for use within the context of the body" (emphasis mine).[9] He includes a spiritual gift questionnaire, which may be helpful as you reevaluate your gifts.

I believe that spiritual gifts can change as our natural gifts mature or new opportunities to use them arise. For example, a mother's gifts of administration and teaching develop as she organizes her home and guides her children wisely. These can be further nurtured to serve the wider body of Christ as she uses them to teach Sunday school or a small group—and maybe even emerge as a gift of mentoring younger women "to prepare God's people for works of service" (Eph. 4:12a).

We may transfer our spiritual gifts from one area of ministry to another. As a gifted teacher my daughter has worked as a children's ministry director for many years. Now those gifts have been fine-tuned and developed so that she teaches other children's leaders all over the country.

A gift of teaching doesn't automatically emerge just because we hold a degree in our hand. Rather, we need to try out our teaching skills and be willing to accept the honest evaluation of others we respect.

We are wise to periodically take time for an internal assessment, especially as we prepare for the major changes ahead. Long before the last child leaves home we should take a serious look at where we're going and prayerfully think through the options before us. Getting away on a personal retreat affords us a block of uninterrupted time to think, pray, and strategize.

A friend of mine had come through several years of pain and loss—the death of her husband, daughters leaving for college, relational difficulties in the small church where she served. She wondered if it was time to "get out and do something else."

Depression was threatening to engulf her, but she had an opportunity to go on a silent prayer retreat in a restful rural area. Long prayer walks and quiet times to read the Bible and listen to what God had to say to her brought great healing and the realization that it wasn't God's time to move on yet.

A silent retreat may be a good time to write out your internal assessment and perhaps even your personal mission statement. In her book *The Path,* author and motivational speaker Laurie Beth Jones takes her readers step-by-step through the process of developing a personal mission statement. She writes, "Having a clear mission statement can help you make decisions in both your work and home. Knowing your personal mission statement is the best career insurance you can have, because once you are clear about what you were put here to do, then 'jobs' become only a means towards your mission, not an end in themselves."[10]

Be Willing to Take Risks

As we enter the second half of life there's an inner excitement about new ideas and opportunities we might pursue, even though trying new things involves risk. Will we make fools of ourselves? Will we fail? Will the cost be worth more than we gain? What can we do that we've never done before?

Perhaps we can try small ventures to test whether or not this is an area we should develop further. Once we've determined what our interests and unique gifts are, we can experiment using them in different ways. Sometimes we are catapulted into change, and then it's much easier if we've had a plan B in mind.

Jean has been interested in antique furniture ever since she inherited a few fine pieces from her grandmother. Over the years, even while working full-time, Jean visited garage sales and antique shows and learned how to assess the resale value of items she purchased. She often picked up bargains while on vacation. When she unexpectedly lost her job she decided to take a risk and began selling antiques through a booth at a retail store. She found that the knowledge she had gained over the years and her appreciation for fine antiques became not only a hobby but a worthwhile investment for her retirement years. She enjoys plan B more than she thought possible.

Thinking creatively about your future may involve going back to school. Over and over the women responding to my questionnaire and focus groups stressed the importance of continuing to learn. Fifteen percent said they had gone back to school or were planning to do so. Gone are the days when a woman over fifty is an oddity in the classroom!

Women can study on the Internet or take single courses at local colleges, either for a credit or just to audit. You can simply follow your intuition or interests to keep mentally alert. Sitting in the classroom will keep you in touch with what younger students are thinking and learning.

Having just overcome a bout with depression, Nancy Schell, now a pastor in California, decided to take a seminary class offered by extension at her church. She felt she needed to get out of herself and try something new, and she took the risk of attending class with younger seminary students. She surprised herself to find she'd fallen in love with the class and became an ardent student of theology.

When she went to tell the professor good-bye after the final class, he asked if she was going to go on. She responded, "I can't. I'm too old. If I go on I have to take Greek and Hebrew." But with the encouragement of her husband and her professor, she continued to take courses, graduated at the age of sixty-three, and has been serving in the church for fifteen years.[11]

Studying not only keeps us in touch with new ideas and avenues of interest, it also keeps us mentally alert. At ninety-four, Supreme Court Justice Oliver Wendell Holmes was asked why he was studying Greek. He responded, "Why, my good sir, it is now or never." Rather than fearing failure, we should look upon learning as an exciting challenge that opens new doors of understanding and makes us more useful in whatever place God has for us down the road.

Learning, of course, does not occur only in the classroom. The love of reading can be developed at any age, and even when eyesight diminishes we can "read" books on tape. Nancy, who works with seniors in her church, found that the women who stay active and alert are the ones who have been reading all their lives.

More than 10 percent of those who responded to my questionnaire had read twenty or more books in the past six months. It's important to include books that broaden our understanding of the world in which we live and expose us to what others are thinking, especially in areas of interest that may be part of our future growth.

Years before I was asked to take the leadership of the AD2000 Women's Track or wrote the book *Women as Risk-Takers for God,* I began to read voraciously on the biblical role of women in the home and in ministry. I found a rich store of books by evangelical authors who led me through in-depth studies of the Scripture and brought me to a new understanding of how God used women in the building of his kingdom. In the past my interest and experience had been with youth and missions, and I had never thought of working with women. But as I read, attended seminars, discussed and prayed over the various issues, I found God had prepared me to accept the leadership of a women's ministry that reached around the world.

Changing careers in the later years is risky, but it can also breathe new vigor into life. With our expanded life expectancy it's possible we'll change careers three, or four, or even more times over the course of our lives.

Associate with People Who Challenge You

One of the advantages of going back to school or attending classes is the opportunity to make new friends and meet people who can broaden our interests. The writer of Proverbs declares, "As iron sharpens iron, so one person sharpens another" (Prov. 27:17 NIVI). While we don't seek friendships primarily to benefit our personal growth, it is helpful to spend time with other women and men who share our interests, who have been successful in areas we are seeking to develop and who are willing to mentor our growth.

When I was a missionary in South Africa my heart was constantly broken by the painful experiences apartheid forced on our African young people. Many of the Christians in the "white" church felt we should not take issue with the government. There was the sense that Christians should not speak out on political issues. The easy way out was to work quietly within the limitations of the system and never express our disapproval.

How thankful I was for several white friends who never settled for this. On occasion I would visit my friend Mary who lived on the other side of Johannesburg. I let her passion and the stories of her experiences with leaders in the cause for justice help keep my own heart aflame for making change happen. She indeed served as "iron sharpening iron" in my life. I believe it is important to cultivate the friendships of those who can stir our imagination and challenge us to think in new directions. Just as we encourage our children to develop friendships that are wholesome and character building, we benefit from relationships with others who challenge our intellectual and spiritual growth.

Practical Stepping-Stones

Dealing with some of the practical issues of aging will not only make this period of life more pleasant but also enable us to squeeze greater meaning and effectiveness out of our lives right to the very end.

Studies show that "good aging" depends to some extent on good health, educational background, and a financial base that allows for basic needs to be met. Though we can't guarantee we'll meet these goals, now is the time to do what we can to achieve them.

In the focus groups I conducted, women acknowledged that they were exercising more, paying more attention to eating nutritionally, and watching their weight. One woman remarked, "I'm taking care of my health so I will not be a burden to anyone." Another expressed gratitude that she had become familiar with the family's finances before her husband died. He had written down everything that had to be paid, including estimated taxes.

Though these suggestions are valid for any stage, this chapter has been speaking primarily to baby boomers who are on the verge of entering the second half of life. As never before, challenge yourself to think creatively, to search for ways to pursue your unfulfilled dreams, to get more training, to network with people who will help you grow, and to take risks to try new ventures. Underlying this preparation for the future, seek constantly to "keep in step with the Spirit," for in the end that's the only way you will finish well.

Highly respected as an educator, our next model, Robyn Claydon, made a Spirit-directed choice in her mid-fifties that drastically turned her life around.

Robyn Claydon

CHOOSING A NEW SECOND HALF

> David and Robyn Claydon have lived in Australia most
> of their lives, but when you read this story you'll realize
> why they've made the world their home.

Robyn walked up the steps to the platform, accompanied by eleven men dressed in somber black suits and by Vera, a young interpreter. She clutched her New Testament tightly, wondering what she should say to the Moscow Baptist Church congregation.

As they moved slowly up the stairs one of the men whispered something to her interpreter. Vera leaned over to Robyn, "He's asked you to give a message." Then she added forcefully, "If he's asked you to give a message, you give a message. We don't have women give messages here."[12]

Sitting on the platform Robyn couldn't see her audience beyond the solid railing that skirted the platform, nor could she understand anything in the service. As she waited to hear the only word she recognized—her name—she reviewed the passage in the first chapter of Philippians, which she'd decided to use.

When the pastor called her name, she and Vera stood together, dwarfed by the high podium. But out in the audience her eyes met an amazing sight. People packed every seat and square foot of standing room in the church. Women comprised most of the audience, "rugged up" as Robyn likes to say in "Australian" against the penetrating cold of the old stone church.

But their faces glowed with inner warmth and anticipation. Robyn had had no idea Russia would be free from communism when she planned her trip here. Freedom had come just two weeks earlier, and worshipers eagerly crowded the three services.

Just a year earlier Robyn had stood with four thousand believers in a stadium in Manila enthusiastically welcoming eighty Russian delegates who had finally been allowed to attend the Lausanne[13] conference there. Even as she rejoiced in their arrival, one week late because of Soviet restrictions, inwardly she pined, "But where are the women?"

Now here she stood, able to tell a packed church how their brothers and sisters around the world had prayed for them. The Holy Spirit gave her a special word as she spoke: "I thank my God every time I remember you. In all my prayers for all of you, I always pray with joy" (Phil. 1:3–4).

Train a Child in the Way . . .

God had prepared Robyn for this ministry from her earliest childhood. Her father served as an Anglican pastor in Sydney, and her mother spoke in churches all over Australia. But rather than leading a separate ministry life, the Hickins included their daughters from the time they were very young.

"We grew up in the church," says Robyn. "My sister and I sat around the kitchen table with our parents as they talked through what they were going to say. We would add our little bits.

"We always went with Mother wherever she spoke, at conferences and youth rallies. We never had a baby-sitter. In those days, instead of an honorarium, you received a handkerchief or a crocheted coat hanger. Of course we heard Dad's sermons on Sundays. We always talked around the kitchen table about what had been said. We experienced this incredible training from the age of about ten right into our twenties."

It may sound incredible to modern ears, but Robyn and her sister, Marlene, loved this family interaction. They often sang hymns together, and the girls learned to harmonize with their parents.

"I used to tell Dad if his sermons were a bit long, 'Dad, I'm going to yawn in twenty minutes.'"

When Robyn's father accepted the pastorate of a historical stone church in a run-down area of Sydney, Robyn's mother took a job singing and playing the organ at a local funeral home so the girls could attend a private church school.

Having grown up in a committed Christian home Robyn says she can't remember when she wasn't a Christian. One night when her dad preached in a country church he brought his message to a conclusion with an invitation. That night when Robyn helped her dad with the dishes she told him, "Daddy, I think I've been converted tonight."

He gently asked her, "Do you believe that you belonged to Jesus from the very beginning?"

She nodded.

"I don't think you were converted tonight. I think you said, 'I want to affirm this for myself,' Robyn."

Robyn accompanied her parents to England where her dad pastored a church for a year. There she began her teaching career even before completing university. Upon the family's return to Australia Robyn taught in a church high school.

"I loved being a teacher. I loved the missionary opportunities. I started a Christian Crusader group in the school and later helped start similar groups in other schools, which became very popular all across Sydney."

Robyn completed her degree at night while she taught school and later earned a master's degree in English literature. She often heard her parents pray for the Christian men their daughters would one day marry. By the time she was twenty-three Robyn admits to being slightly anxious, wondering where this man was that her parents had been praying for all these years.

"There was no one out there who interested me at all."

Because of their willingness to serve in missions, Robyn and her sister joined a youth group of the CMS (Church Missionary Society). They went to a CMS camp where they didn't know anybody. The first morning Marlene got up early for kitchen duty, leaving Robyn to sleep in. But she returned very quickly to shake her awake.

"Rob, Rob, you've got to get up to see this gorgeous boy in his yellow jumper [sweater]." Robyn wasn't the least interested and leisurely prepared for the day. But when she saw him, she had to admit that this guy with his lovely shock of curly red hair and canary yellow jumper intrigued her.

Before the camp ended, the leaders formed a leadership committee on which both Marlene and Robyn agreed to serve and the "gorgeous" David Claydon was asked to be president. They worked together on CMS projects, and when Christmas came, Robyn discovered that David had no family to go home to. With her mother's approval she sent David a note: "If you're free on Christmas Day we'd like to have you for lunch."

David rang up to say he had other plans but wondered about New Year's Eve. He came, looking gorgeous in a navy blue blazer, and Robyn lost her heart. Three weeks later when he returned from a CMS camp he'd led, he dropped in unexpectedly to see her. In the meantime Robyn had contracted chicken pox from her students, and though she was no longer contagious, she didn't look her best, to say the least, to welcome him.

Over the next year David and Robyn saw a lot of each other. He often invited her to the International Hostel at the university where he lived with students from all over Asia and which contributed to his lifelong love for Asian people.

Gradually Robyn learned of David's background. Born in Bethlehem to English civil servants, David had lost both his parents in a skirmish between the Palestinians, Zionists, and British when he was an infant. For a time he lived in an orphanage where he learned Arabic as his first language. When the home closed, missionaries took him in, until a single CMS missionary, Lora Claydon, came to Jerusalem from Ethiopia and looked after David. She became his permanent guardian and gave him her name. However, she would not allow him to speak Arabic—she wanted him to be a proper English boy.

Auntie Lora worked for a time in Jerusalem, and David lived with her in the caretaker's house in the garden tomb. Eager to leave the politically unstable region, Lora looked for a ship going either to England or Australia, where she had relatives. In 1944 the government arranged for Lora and David to go to Egypt and eventually on a troop ship to Australia.

Even though he was only nine years old, David remembers the ship zigzagging across the Indian Ocean through the night to avoid the enemy. On one occasion he was sent to bed because there was a German U-boat in the area; meanwhile, the adults stayed up all night to pray for safety.

Balancing Home and Career

After a year's engagement, Robyn and David married in 1961. In the Australian school system grades eleven and twelve comprise one unit for testing, and Robyn wanted to wait to see her students through the exams. That year David became the Field Director for Scripture Union. A few years later he became the National Director with responsibilities in the South Pacific and Southeast Asia. He ministered in Scripture Union for twenty-one years.

Fifteen months after their marriage, daughter Kim joined their family. Though Robyn and David longed for more children, it was not to be. Once Kim was old enough for school Robyn returned to teaching, taking her daughter with her. When the family moved, they wanted Kim to go to a school near their home and asked the "head" of Abbotsleigh Girls School to allow Kim to attend there.

Abbotsleigh is a leading girls' school in Australia and gets the top academic results every year. Many parents register their daughters at birth to ensure a place for them, so Robyn was delighted that the school had space for Kim. Financially she could afford it only because she was teaching. A year later Abbotsleigh needed a deputy vice-principal and appointed Robyn to this position.

For the next eighteen years Robyn worked at the school, first as a deputy and then as vice-principal. "I loved it and I never thought that I would give it up. It was in my blood," Robyn asserts. "I loved teaching English and the opportunity for Christian witness. I would have taught at Abbotsleigh without being paid, if I didn't need money for Kim's education."

The years on Abbotsleigh's stately campus with its historical red brick buildings resonated with growth and challenge. Robyn filled diverse responsibilities and besides teaching, she spoke in chapel and dealt with any discipline problems.

"These students came from homes where education is prized, so they worked," she explains. "Abbotsleigh has twelve hundred girls from kindergarten through high school and very few disciplinary problems."

She remembers only one time when a girl came to her, fearing that she was pregnant. Robyn offered to take her to her own personal doctor for a test. When they learned that the results were negative, Robyn queried her, "Can you imagine the consequences if the results had been different? I would have had to ring your parents. You would have had to leave school." A trust relationship developed, and the girl often visited Robyn's office in the future for advice and counsel.

Robyn pioneered a program for personal development, which was used in a number of schools throughout Australia. When she visited private schools in the U.S. in 1983, she found that teachers eagerly received the textbook she had written on the subject.

A Turning Point

In 1985 Abbotsleigh celebrated its hundredth anniversary, and Robyn wrote an eight-scene pageant of the school's history, which included every student in the school. She also wrote the closing song, which became the school song. Her little granddaughter Georgia could sing it lustily even before she began kindergarten there in 2000.

After the anniversary celebrations, Robyn felt life would finally return to normal. But one day she received a phone call from California. A minister invited her to serve on the planning committee for a Lausanne conference to be held in Manila in 1989. They needed someone from each of ten regions. "We're keen to have you because we need a woman on the committee, and you'll be the only one," he confessed.

Robyn discovered later that Leighton Ford, the director of the Lausanne Committee, had recommended her. Ford had met Robyn more than ten years earlier when he conducted a campaign in Sydney and she helped with puppet and drama presentations for him. She invited him to speak at Abbotsleigh to the students and staff. Robyn recalls with embarrassment that she told him, "If you ever need a woman to speak in women's meetings in your crusades, I'd love to do that." He didn't respond to that offer, but now he was asking her to represent all of the South Pacific countries in an international conference.

The Passion Begins

What a thrill to see a thousand gifted women leaders participating in the Manila conference. A representative team from each of ten countries put on a daily two-hour women's session at the ten-day conference. They were given no particular theme, but over and over women raised the issue of their lack of opportunity to serve. Repeatedly Robyn heard, "We're not being used; we want to be in team leadership with men; we would like to be allowed to use all our ministry gifts." They wanted to look at Scriptures to see how they could counteract some of the false interpretations. At last they had an opportunity to express their feelings.

Returning home to her job at Abbotsleigh, Robyn could not get these women out of her mind. She had gotten to know many of them well and wondered how she could help them.

But when Leighton Ford called to invite her to become a Lausanne Senior Associate for Women, Robyn was dumbfounded.

He asked her to consider networking around the world, speaking, preaching, and encouraging women to be God's person. That sounded exciting, but his next words brought her up short. "We can't pay you. You'd have to raise your own expenses. You may have to leave your teaching job."

Initially Robyn told him no. But as she thought and prayed about it and talked it over with her family, it began to make sense, for she had to admit the women had captured her heart. Kim had married the year before, and David now served as director of CMS and had many overseas commitments, so Robyn was freer to consider a role that involved a lot of traveling. But her teaching salary surpassed David's, and if she took her retirement now at fifty-five, it would mean a big drop in income.

From the beginning David encouraged her to step out by faith. He felt sure they could manage financially, especially since CMS provided their housing.

Even as she tested God by asking him to give her peace to say no, the needs and opportunities to serve women globally never strayed far from her mind. "I never lost my desire for teaching," she reiterates. "I found myself thinking, Lord, I've only got ten more years. But instead the Lord kept bringing up all those other possibilities. By June I was convinced that if I stayed with my teaching job I would be constantly thinking of the opportunities out there that I hadn't taken."

In mid-1990 she turned in her resignation and began planning her first trip. But where should she go first? Since many countries had been freed from communism in 1989 she felt the former Soviet nations needed her help the most. She wrote to the women she had met from Czech Republic, Romania, Poland, and Russia, but very few responded. When she actually purchased her ticket for Russia she did not know if anyone had arranged meetings or if they'd even received her letters.

Her fears were unfounded, for her contact in Moscow, Vera, had arranged one meeting after another, and women eagerly drank in her teaching and appreciated the Russian Bibles she'd brought.

Since accepting the role as the Lausanne Senior Associate for Women, Robyn has spoken in over fifty countries, from Nepal to South Africa. She goes everywhere with only one small carry-on case, no matter if the trip is for a weekend or a month. Seeing her various coordinated combinations is as bewildering as watching a magician pulling a menagerie out of a hat. How does she do it?

During the first year Robyn paid for all her expenses out of her pension but soon realized she couldn't keep that up. As she told of her call and travels in meetings in Australia, people began asking if they could help her. Now at the beginning of each year she figures out where she will go in the next year, what it will cost, and presents that to a small number of interested friends. Generally the gifts cover the expenses with nothing left over.

There've been tests along the way—David's heart surgery to replace a defective valve and her breast cancer surgery in 1998. She learned of the positive biopsy on the way to the airport to go to a women's convention in Germany. God gave her the grace to speak at the meetings even with that shadow hanging over her. Five years after the surgery she was clear of cancer.

Following Her Passion

Mentoring has become one of Robyn's primary passions. "I see so many able young women as I travel around the world. After leading a conference in Germany in 2000 for eighteen young women leaders from around the world and six older mentors, I keep in touch with them and visit them in their country if I can. I listen to them speak and give them lots of encouragement."

In her seminars Robyn teaches that a good mentor:

Is prepared to listen
Asks the right questions
Is more interested in the other person than themselves
Is willing to be vulnerable

Trusts and can be trusted; keeps confidences

Knows and loves the Lord and has a passion to share the gospel

Knows the Scriptures well

Is willing to be helped as much as to help

When asked whether she feels her sixty-eight years she replied, "I've felt about thirty-five as long as I can remember. I guess since I still have my health I don't feel like I'm getting old."

Roles continue to change in the Claydon family. In 2001 Robyn was asked to serve on the Lausanne International Committee as vice-chairperson. In 2002 David retired from CMS and became the International Director of Lausanne. So at last David and Robyn travel and minister together frequently.

Robyn wrote in her latest book, *Keep Walking,* "As we keep walking and as we face tomorrow with all its challenges and uncertainties, may we fix our eyes on Jesus and re-dedicate ourselves for whatever lies ahead, because we have not walked this way before!"[14]

FIVE

PREPARING FOR DIFFICULT TRANSITIONS

"For I know the plans I have for you," declares the Lord, "plans to prosper you and not to harm you, plans to give you hope and a future."

Jeremiah 29:11

Plan ahead—it wasn't raining when Noah built the ark.

Internet

Transitions and changes can be exciting or terrifying; either way they cause stress. Think of the changes most of us have gone through—we started school, graduated, landed our first job, broke up with a boyfriend, were married, had our first baby—on and on. Each change brought a certain amount of discomfort and fear as we adapted to new demands on our inner self. In each new situation we left something behind, which brought about a period of discomfort and disorientation until we were comfortable with the new stage in life.

In 1993 my husband and I moved from California to Colorado so we could be closer to the AD2000 & Beyond offices. The decision to do so was relatively easy since it enabled us to work more closely with the leaders of the movement. But the transition was stressful.

Selling our house became a long, drawn-out process with cantankerous buyers. Leaving family including three grand-children was traumatic. Saying good-bye to our church family and a Bible study group with whom we'd shared our lives for seventeen years was painful.

Once settled in our new home we relished the pure air of Colorado Springs and reveled in the beauty of the mountains. We had to start over—find a doctor, hairdresser, bank; look for a church, Sunday school class, and Bible study group to plug into; make new friends. It took at least five years before we felt like "Coloradoans," and the bumper stickers saying, "Now that you've seen Colorado, go back to California" didn't help. Changing from a salaried position to living on social security and gifts from donors brought its own set of challenges.

We were both over sixty-five and had experienced many changes over the years, which enabled us to face yet another one. We knew full well the risks we were taking, and we also were confident that God was leading.

When God puts our lives into a "change mode" we need to be ready to "keep in step with the Spirit." Sometimes we resist change and get stuck on a plateau. Bob Buford warns:

> When you're on a "paradigm plateau," your identity is on autopilot—you're in a groove with habits and practices that earned you success and respect. . . . The problem here is that you overstay the party and become almost a caricature of your-self. Eventually you become like the boxer who keeps fighting beyond his prime.[1]

Often the older we get the more difficult it is to step out of our comfortable routine into a new challenging experience. How easily we get set in our ways!

Stressful as changes of career or places to live may be, we can choose to deal with them under the Spirit's direction. We are normally involved in the decision-making process. But the transitions we will discuss in this chapter come generally not by choice or design. Though most are inevitable, they will require life preparation if we are to meet them with dignity and peace.

Life Preparation

Life preparation involves the disciplines of the Christian walk. These bring us to spiritual maturity so we are prepared to face whatever experiences lie ahead. As we intentionally seek maturity we'll find greater strength to face change. We aim for growth rather than stalled character development, where we are unable or unwilling to deal with negative personality traits. The Scriptures urge: "Run after mature righteousness—faith, love, peace—joining those who are in honest and sincere prayer before God" (2 Tim. 2:22 MESSAGE).

Daily commitment to reading the Word of God for the purpose of seeking his guidance for life's decisions is basic. This is the secret: "Through the Word we are put together and shaped up for the tasks God has for us" (2 Tim. 3:17 MESSAGE).

But it takes more than this! Ethel Herr, author of *Lord Show Me Your Glory,*[2] reminded me that just reading the Word for guidance is not enough; we must live in the Word in our search for God himself.

"You must live a life of walking so close to God that his glory is your ultimate desire and goal and you are able to trust him implicitly with all the complexities and mysteries of life you can never understand," she told me.

My husband and I visited an old friend who had lost his wife and his job in a short period of time. When asked what God is teaching him these days he quietly responded, "I'm learning to trust God." He had just discovered that his only son has ALS.[3] He was clinging to such promises in God's Word as: "Surely God is my help; the Lord is the one who sustains me" (Ps. 54:4).

We must internalize trust in God to sustain us in any circumstance if we are to be prepared for the inevitable transitions ahead. Trust must become a solid core of our lives so we can face the future with peace, as the apostle Paul did: "The One I've trusted in can take care of what he's trusted me to do right to the end" (2 Tim. 1:12 MESSAGE).

Tough Transitions Ahead

What are the tough transitions that most of us will face in the second half of our lives? How will they affect our perceptions of ourselves? You may have already passed through some of these stages, but for baby boomers most challenges still lie ahead and will change their perception of who they are. Each transition to a new stage of life affects our relationship with others:

I am needed by others	Children, husband Aging parents Colleagues at work, clients, patients Neighbors
I am no longer needed by others	Empty nest Job loss Retirement Widowhood Divorce
I need others	Physical frailty Care receiver Nursing home

In his book *Transitions* William Bridges describes life's transitions as "an ending . . . followed by a period of confusion and distress . . . leading to a new beginning."[4] Endings are difficult; it's hard to let go of the past where we knew who we were and what to expect. Each ending brings its own sense of grief and loss, especially when the next step is shrouded in darkness. But even when we know we are going on to better things, loss is loss. Death is the final ending—but for believers it signifies a new beginning with the promise of no more losses.

The Holding Zone

Bridges reminds us that "before we can find a new something, we must deal with a time of nothing."[5] This transition stage or holding zone may be a time of emptiness, pain, grief, confusion, bewilderment, fear, and uncertainty. After a major change or loss we may find ourselves longing for the past, unable to concentrate or enjoy new activities. In this time of unreality we need to recognize it is a temporary state. It is longer for some than others, but with God's help, we will come through it. Here in this gaping space our core of trust grows vital.

More than ever in these times we need to be alone with God, bare our hearts to the One who truly understands our pain, and listen to his voice. Many find keeping a journal of a transition experience helps them to make more sense out of it.

Our son Randy spent the last six weeks of his life in intensive care. His wife kept a daily journal of his roller-coaster experience—one day hope because his vital signs improved, the next despair as an infection set in. She carefully recorded Randy's words in his brief intervals of awareness. Sharing that journal with the rest of the family after his death helped us all to bring closure to this painful loss.

As in any ending, the love and concern of friends helps make the transition easier. This is part of the unique design of the body of Christ, and we need to be sensitive to those around us who are experiencing an ending—even a good one! A concerned phone call or simply the assurance "I've been praying for you" penetrates the sense of emptiness.

The Empty Nest

Having our children leave home for good can be painful. Even though we teach them to be independent—to drive, get a part-time job, and go away to college—we still have a deep sense of loss when they leave. We are still mothers but no longer mommies. Gone are the days when our children ran in with a bruised knee or an A on their spelling paper. No more phone calls to interrupt our dinner. No more parent-teacher conferences or running soccer taxi. We don't wait up for our teenagers to return from a date, starry-eyed and full of questions.

Of course, we want to let them go. We encourage their independence and continue to pray fervently for them. The emptiness will pass. For many women this is the transition into a richer second half of life.

I will always remember walking through our house in Africa the first time after leaving our two eldest sons in college in America. Their school uniforms still hung in the closet; their beds were neatly made; their schoolbooks lay on the shelf. My stomach knotted up with an indescribable pain, and I wondered how I would stand the silence without Mark's trumpet practice or Nathan strumming his guitar. At that moment I couldn't even imagine what richness lay ahead in ministry and travel.

The empty nest will probably not take you by surprise. If you've been wise in anticipating this move, you'll have already developed new interests, hobbies, or skills, and worked on an ever-closer relationship with your husband. Perhaps now you will find more time for in-depth Bible study and intercessory prayer, or improving your computer skills, or taking courses at the local college. You might even start a new career. Once the sense of loss passes (and it will) you will see an unexpected door open, beckoning you into one of the richest times of your life.

When Parents Need Help

As far back as the fifth commandment in Exodus 20, the Bible clearly states that we are to honor and care for our parents by loving them, respecting them, and even taking responsibility financially if needed. "If a widow has family members to take care of her, let them learn that religion begins at their own doorstep and that they should pay back with gratitude some of what they have received" (1 Tim. 5:4 MESSAGE).

Care goes far beyond finances. Parents long for love, warm hugs, and the friendship of their children as the years deprive them of physical strength, long-term friendships, and opportunities to do meaningful work.

Today medical ethicists debate about who should receive expensive medical treatment and when care should be restricted because of quality of life or excessive costs. Abortion, cloning, and euthanasia advocates come perilously close to defining human life as valueless if it is "nonproductive."

Non-Christian cultures deal with caring for the elderly in different ways. When asked who should receive available resources, the Akamba healers of Kenya responded with what seemed obvious to them—their elders. Their society puts so much value on the contributed wisdom and experience of their elderly that they consider them the most important people in the tribe.

People in some cultures kill their elderly. Stephen Post, professor in the School of Medicine at Case Western University, tells of well-documented practices in Japan where the oldest son of a parent in an advanced stage of dementia buries his parent's head in a bowl of water as an act of filial piety.[6]

For Christians of any society, human life has immeasurable value because we are created in the image of God. Even when we are frail, demented, and seemingly nonproductive, Jesus says we have value. "Look at the birds of the air; they do not *sow* or *reap* or *store away* in barns, and yet your heavenly Father feeds them. Are you not much more valuable than they?" (Matt. 6:26, emphasis mine).

Caring for elderly parents may take many forms. We moved my depressed mother from Milwaukee to an apartment in California so I could be near enough to give her the love and attention she needed.

Friends of mine purchased a home with a comfortable self-contained lower level so their parents could live independently but know family was there for them.

While most elderly parents have at least social security income, many do not have the means to care for themselves, especially in the light of rising health costs. Loving Christian families will be aware of their parents' needs and will help as best they can.

Diane's mother insists on staying in her own mobile home, many miles from her daughter. Between Diane, her brother, and their uncle, they pool their resources to subsidize her mother's income so she can remain independent as long as possible.

One of the most difficult decisions is to place an elderly parent in a nursing home against his or her wishes. If you've had to do that you will identify with the story of Blanche in chapter 9.

Many women find themselves in the sandwich generation— stretched between the needs of their own children and caring for their elderly parents. Often they are holding down a full-time job as well. The results of my questionnaire indicated that 10 percent of the women who responded were overwhelmed by caring for their aged parents.

How can you prepare for the possibility of caring for elderly parents especially if you've had a difficult relationship over the years? Unfortunately many today have negative attitudes about their parents, perhaps even justifiably so. But as we grow in character and spiritual maturity, we will develop the biblical attitude toward our parents—an attitude of gratitude, love, responsibility, and honor. We will take time to recognize *their* needs, not only materially (if necessary) but also for a closer relationship with us, their children, and for sensitivity when strength and mental abilities decline.

As daughters, we are most likely to end up with the responsibility for caring for our parents—and even our in-laws. A friend of mine cared for her ailing parents in her home until they died, and then she cared for her mother-in-law who was dying of cancer. But God honored my friend's faithfulness and since then has given her twenty more years of serving him in a rich teaching ministry.

One way to prepare for the care of our parents is to work on family togetherness with siblings now, keeping in regular touch with each other. With families so scattered these days, it's helpful to maintain telephone and email connections, though nothing takes the place of face-to-face visits and the opportunity to see for ourselves how our parents are doing. It's not enough to tell your brother or sister that Mother seems to be getting frail; they need to see it for themselves. And the family ought to talk over possibilities of their parents moving from their large house or needing additional medical treatment.

Many families do not discuss these changes or know their parents' financial situation until the crisis comes upon them. Suddenly the son or daughter must reverse roles and make decisions *for* their parents rather than *with* them. Scrambling through paperwork and trying to decide if Mother can afford a recommended nursing home in the urgency of the situation can be avoided if open financial discussions have taken place.

Marge's husband, George, has Alzheimer's (another caregiving situation we may face). Marge and her three sons have worked together as a team to ease her difficult responsibility. Her son Jim and his wife, who were living in another town, found new jobs and bought a home within a few miles of his parents' home. Jim and his brothers took turns relieving Marge of her daily caregiving.

When George fell and broke his hip Marge knew she could no longer care for him at home. Because they had wisely purchased long-term insurance some years earlier, two-thirds of George's nursing home costs were covered. This enabled Marge and her sons to select a well-established and comfortable nursing home just a few minutes' drive from her house.

In an open family relationship you can encourage your parents to take care of such matters as their will, a medical power of attorney for health care decisions, or long-term care insurance (if they have the means to do so).[7] Most of us do not realize the importance of long-term care, or that it is *not* covered by Medicare. The average eighty-year-old woman can now anticipate another seven to ten years of life, and with the costs of long-term care rising incrementally, she can expect to spend $125,000 if she goes into a nursing home.[8]

One way to diplomatically alert your parents to this possibility (and for the good of all concerned) is to have your own will and insurance in order and share this with your parents. According to the AARP, among Americans fifty and older, only 17 percent have a will, a durable power of attorney, and a living trust.[9] When you tell your parents what you've done about your own affairs, they may more easily see that it's time for them to do the same.

While we can encourage parents to take care of insurance and legal matters, dealing with personal property is a more sensitive issue and may even trigger a family feud. Once again your own actions may encourage your parents to follow suit. One suggestion may be to put stickers with the names of family members on valuable items or ask children directly what they would like to have and make a written record. As long as we refuse to face the eventual reality of death—which for the believer should have lost its sting—parents and children find it difficult to discuss these matters. Experts say that "'parents need to be parents one last time.' . . . It's the final statement you make as a parent. Done openly, it will ensure the greatest legacy of all: family members who remain friends after you're gone."[10]

Preparing for Retirement

Whatever our primary role in life, at some point retirement becomes an issue—either by choice or by force. Hopefully we will begin to plan for retirement long before it happens. We generally think of retirement as reaching a point in life when we step out of our routine career or job to enjoy the leisure of doing only what we want to do. *Retirement* actually means "withdrawal, or being out of circulation." It has been described as a "roleless role." It's the ending we both look forward to and dread, and we may put it off as long as we can.

Nowhere does the Bible speak of retirement. While the Levites were told to relinquish their official responsibilities at fifty, they continued to serve as mentors to younger priests

(Num. 8:25–26). We see Anna still ministering in the temple well into her eighties or more, and we believe that John wrote Revelation on the Isle of Patmos in his nineties.

The concept of official retirement is fairly recent. In 1899 German Chancellor Otto Bismarck established sixty-five as the age when his government would begin paying retirement pensions. Since life expectancy was only about fifty-five at the time, he felt fairly safe that no one would live long enough to claim benefits.

In the United States the Social Security Act of 1935 set the age of retirement at sixty-five, which was intended to ease the older workers out of the workplace, making room for younger unemployed workers. This was seen as a partial solution to the unemployment lines of the Depression.

With the shorter life span of the early twentieth century, few expected to reach the golden age of retirement. Even Franklin Roosevelt, the designer of the program, died at age sixty-three and did not live long enough to enjoy the benefits of social security.

But with the extended second half of life, retirement can become a long empty look into less and less. Dr. Howard G. Hendricks quotes Norman Cousins: "Retirement, supposed to be a chance to join the winners' circle, has turned out to be more dangerous than automobiles or LSD. . . . It is the chance to do everything that leads to nothing. It is the gleaming brass ring that unhorses the rider." Hendricks concludes, "The reason is clear: There are two lines in a person's life; the lifeline and the purpose line. When the purpose line evaporates, it is just a matter of time before the lifeline ceases."[11]

The longing for purpose infuses our heart so that we feel urgent about finding the next step. We keep looking for the plan God has for us, and we panic at the fear of empty days ahead. Is it any wonder that so many women express a sense of trepidation as they contemplate the possible longevity before them?

Numerous studies have shown that women who have crea- tive and challenging jobs find retirement more difficult than those who had mediocre job satisfaction. These career women lose not only the stimulation of their work but also what they consider their identity.

A spouse's retirement can also prove a difficult change. A cartoon in our local newspaper pictured a man slouching over the kitchen table reading the newspaper while his wife calls the police, saying, "I want to report a bum who's been loitering around my house."

Rather than dreading the thought of a man around the house all day to interrupt your comfortable schedule, you can begin now to talk about how to develop ways to serve, exercise, play, and share responsibilities *together*. What an opportunity to make an exciting and meaningful beginning, planning for some of the unfulfilled dreams you had as a young couple, before children, mortgage, and career responsibilities!

Lack of adequate finances can make retirement difficult. It's important to plan ahead, and it's never too soon to start investing for retirement. But money should not be the prime concern. Retirees need to find something that matters deeply to them to give them purpose. Some of the most contented women I met in my research had very little income, but they had a heart and passion to love God and serve others.

We want to please our husbands and enjoy their interests with them, and so we should. But we also need to develop our own gifts and interests, become whole persons in our own right, and understand who we are in Christ—his special daughters. This not only prepares us for future loss but also makes us a more stimulating and challenging life companion as we grow old together.

You'll notice from the list of activities women are pursuing in preparation for their bonus years (see p. 99) that many are self-improvements. Whether it's studying the Bible for spiritual development, attending college to prepare for a possible career change, or a short-term missions trip toward a new ministry, they are learning new things for future use. This in turn develops a healthy sense of independence and self-confidence, which will stand us in good stead in the time of loss. A woman who has always depended on her husband for every decision and has never developed her own abilities faces a double loss when her husband dies. She's lost her life's companion as well as her own identity.

Can We Prepare for the Loss of Loved Ones?

"Widowhood is a kind of retirement," says renowned psychologist Paul Tournier, "the retirement of the woman from her job as a wife."[12]

And most married women will face that retirement, for the average married woman lives another seventeen years after her husband dies.[13]

In many ways none of us can ever prepare for the tearing loss of widowhood. A friend described her feelings as though she had been cut in half. Some people who have experienced both death of a spouse and divorce say that divorce can be more painful partly because of the difficulty to bring closure to the relationship. But in either case, we try not to think about these changes in life, somehow hoping that by our denial they will never take place.

The statistics are brutal:

36 percent of women between sixty-five and seventy-four are widows,

62 percent over seventy-five.[14]

More than one-third of women over sixty-five live alone.[15]

The divorce rate for fifty-year-old women is 24 percent.[16]

With this stark reality, we would be wise to think about being ready for loss. Even with the best of preparations grief must take its course. General wisdom indicates that it takes an average of two years to grieve daily after the loss of a loved one.

My friend tells of going into the closet and burrowing her face in the familiar smell of her husband's sweater so that no one could hear her screams. Another woman would get into her car and drive and drive, dreading to return home to an empty house. Even five years after my son's untimely death I fight unbidden tears if we sing a song that was sung at his funeral.

April Holthaus wrote these memories in her widows' newsletter, *Survivors Hope,* ten years after her husband passed away suddenly:

> Ten years today! Can it possibly be that long ago that I found your lifeless body on the floor of our bedroom and you were already in heaven?
>
> My first thought was, how could the years have passed so quickly when I was aware so often that I was alone. **Alone!** At first, I had the awful task of learning to pay the bills and taxes and make all the decisions that go with trying to be financially responsible. **Alone**—to make huge decisions about buying and selling houses. **Alone** to try to talk myself out of being afraid of so many of those big decisions—buying a car, moving, investing your insurance payoffs, selling our possessions or initially giving away your personal things.
>
> As I went to Scripture in those times of fear and doubt and loneliness, I learned to stand on God's promise that he would be "a husband and provider to the widow and father to the fatherless."
>
> But hon, it took me a few years to realize that the deepest hurt of my heart was because I wasn't *special* to anyone anymore. No special someone to live with me and excuse my deepest faults. No someone I could intimately trust with my opinions and scary thoughts, or battle out life's issues with.
>
> I had the comfort of many dear friends and my wonderful family. Thank goodness I am a pretty outgoing person who enjoys the company of others and has many interests in the areas of art, music, biblical archaeology, nature photography and travel.
>
> But it wasn't until I looked into completing my education that God began to grow me up inside. Completing a BS in Management gave me contacts with others who also desired to better their lives.

> Today I can look back at the past ten years. I'm still alone. . . . I'm still wondering what my future holds. But the biggest change has been in experiencing a daily personal dependence on God. Possibly if I still relied on you for so many of my decisions and security this strong relationship with my heavenly Father would not be as dynamic as it is today.[17]

While we continue to miss our loved ones, we can prepare to help heal the pain. In Tournier's masterful book *Learning to Grow Old,* he writes, "One can live for God from one's youth up, and that I have no doubt, is the best preparation for old age."[18] And the best preparation for life's losses.

When April's husband died suddenly she had never balanced a checkbook. She dreaded facing the bills that were piling up, for her husband had always taken care of all their finances. Nancy (see chapter 7) was shocked to learn of her newfound wealth after her husband divorced her and their assets were divided. She was fortunate to have sons to help her wade through the financial process.

In a healthy marriage relationship both members are fully aware of their income and expenses, their assets and liabilities. You need to know if you will be financially independent should you be left alone. What are your mutual wishes concerning leaving money to your heirs or to kingdom work? Will you need to work? Do you have job experience? Do you need more training?

After her husband left her for another woman, Fran found that she couldn't maintain the house and care for her four children without going to work. "Looking for a job at forty-five was embarrassing," she says. "I had no skills or recent experience. It really made me lose any self-esteem I had."

We've already referred to the importance of having an updated will and a willing executor. It's difficult to discuss final arrangements such as cremation versus burial because we tend to avoid speaking about the inevitable. But having plans written out, such as favorite hymns or who should perform the memorial service, makes it much easier for those left behind.

Placing your assets in a revocable trust will save probate costs and simplifies handling all the legal details. While my husband and I divide financial responsibilities—he pays the monthly bills and keeps our checking account in balance; I handle investments—we periodically sit down and discuss our finances. I make sure he knows where the key to the bank deposit and the investment statements are, and he keeps me informed of the status of our account.

Paul Tournier's writings about growing old together ring sweetly from his own experience. At ninety he commiserates with those who have to live alone in contrast to what he calls his own "privileged state" of marriage. He writes, "This blessing of being able to grow old together is the fruit of a whole married life in which one has been given the courage to face, in a dialogue of truth, a host of problems of mutual adaptation which are never easy. It is as true of a couple as it is of an individual, that old age depends mainly upon the way their lives have been lived beforehand."[19]

When relationships are troubled, loss becomes even more difficult. When Dr. Laura Schlesinger's mother's murdered body was found, it appeared she'd been dead for some time. Weeks later the opinionated and sometimes abrasive on-air counselor appeared on the *Larry King Live* program to respond to questions about her loss. Though she and her mother had been estranged for twenty years, it was obvious the shock of her death had deeply affected Dr. Laura. Usually very sure of herself, she found it difficult to control her voice or hold back tears. The estrangement and circumstances leading up to it had compounded her loss and intensified her grief. She had not been able to deal with unfinished business before her mother was killed.

When our marriage is deeply satisfying, marked by intimate and loving companionship, it may intensify our fear of losing our beloved. But Tournier and others confirm that those who have been closest in marriage bear their separation best. "The most unconsolable sorrows are those kept alive by a guilty conscience," says Tournier.[20] Loss will leave a hole in our heart, but if we make a Christ-honoring marriage a high priority, that hole can be filled with warm memories without regrets or guilt.

Doris Waldrop had to face the possibility of loss when her husband, Bill, left for Vietnam. He warned her to get all their affairs in order because he might not come back. After flying two hundred missions he returned safely, but Doris had learned a valuable lesson for the future.

Later, following a busy pastorate, Bill became the leader of a para-church organization and traveled a lot. In search of an anchor for her drifting spirit, Doris began working on a master's degree in counseling. She was already in her fifties and had never used a computer. Whenever she spoke of giving it up Bill urged her to finish.

As Bill neared retirement they planned to travel and pursue their hobby of bird watching. But their lives came to an abrupt end when Bill suddenly died of a heart attack.

A new grandchild, born just weeks after Bill's death, helped to fill some of the void. But about six months later Doris felt it was time to get on with her life. She knew that Bill would want her to continue to use her skills and the training that he had been so anxious for her to complete. It seemed as though God had given her this painful experience so she could share it with young women in the military—wives and mothers whose husbands and sons were often gone from home for long periods of time.

Doris's eyes sparkle as she talks about the opportunities before her to mentor young women, to train leadership, and to share God's faithfulness as he's brought her through her loss.

"God has revealed himself in so many ways since I'm walking alone," she explains. And it's this truth she wants to impart to younger women who also face "aloneness" in different ways.[21]

The Life of Faith

The best preparation for our tough transitions is the life of faith and trust, growing in confidence that God loves us and will always be with us. We referred earlier to life preparation—the walk of faith that builds our mature character and makes us more Christlike. You'll see such a walk of faith modeled in the life of Mavis Nkosi in the next section. Eugene Peterson described this kind of walk as "a long obedience in the same direction."

We've spoken of trust as the core of our walk. Trust enables us to say "Your will be done" even when our hearts cry "Why?" Trust enables us to cling to God's love even when fear grips our hearts. Trust assures us that our dying loved one (or our empty nest, or our threatened divorce, or . . .) is secure in God's sovereign care even while our souls cry "No." Trust enables us to believe that the darkness clutching our heart will lift and that joy will once again be a reality.

Mavis Nkosi

A Burden That Won't Let Go

Mavis and Jerry Nkosi cofounded a youth ministry with an American missionary couple in the black township outside of Johannesburg, South Africa. After leading the ministry for twelve years they felt called to reach inner-city youth in Dallas, Texas—a totally different challenge.

When Mavis Nkosi looks back on the months after her husband's death, she knows only God's grace and sustaining strength kept her going. She had cared for Jerry for five years, through two heart attacks and two strokes, which left him weepy and physically unstable.

Shortly after Jerry's death in 1994 Mavis discovered that her daughter Lena was succumbing to a problem with alcohol. Lena was losing her home and couldn't care for her two sons, Cory and Cameron. So Mavis invited Lena and the boys to move in with her to give the boys some stability. But the drinking problem increased, and a few months later Mavis felt she had no other recourse but to ask Lena to leave.

"It was difficult," she remembers. "I was still trying to deal with Jerry's passing; I was exhausted and at the time I was fully responsible for the ministry in a Dallas housing development. And now at age sixty-seven I had two children to take care of—a teenager and a three-year-old toddler." But smiling she adds, "It took my mind off my pain and gave me something to do."[22]

Growing Up in South Africa

Mavis wanted the boys to have the stability and Christian teaching she'd had growing up in a Zulu community in South Africa. The Sokhela family lived on a small farm, raising vegetables they sold at the local market. Her father also held a job with the railway, which helped to pay for the care and education of eight children, of whom Mavis was the youngest. Their simple three-bedroom home had no electricity or running water, and the girls carried all their water from the river back to the house in buckets on their heads.

Her father had become a Christian while working for an American missionary, and over time his whole family became believers, including a sister who had been a witch doctor. Mavis remembers happy, loving times together when the whole extended family gathered for prayer meetings on Sunday mornings before church. Though the family had financial difficulties, her father encouraged the children to go to high school, and three of the girls became teachers and one a nurse, which was unusual for a rural African family.

The apartheid system of the country offered teaching and nursing as the only two career options open to African girls. Mavis knew from a very young age that she wanted to be a teacher. Even though apartheid limited Africans' freedom, Mavis didn't let it deter her.

"You didn't think much about it because there was no way to get rid of it. The hardest thing was the everyday put-down. I wasn't into being radical and displaying discontent," she says. But she sadly comments that it was "Christians who brainwashed Christians. We were told it was sinful to say anything against the government. We were given the impression that you had to go along with it. . . . Even some of the missionaries knowingly or unknowingly bought into the system."

With some additional training in domestic science after Teacher Training College, Mavis taught at ETTC (Evangelical Teacher Training College). There she helped start a Friday night youth meeting in the local township with an American missionary couple. Hundreds of kids flocked to the town hall to play games, watch movies for the first time in their lives, and hear Bible teaching directed straight at their hearts. Mavis remembers that the kids who couldn't get in often pelted stones on the metal roof so that it sounded like a hailstorm inside.

When ETTC closed its domestic science classes Mavis left, hoping to get a job nearer home. One day she received a letter from her oldest sister, Greta, telling about a need for a teacher in Egazini, a remote area on the border of Zululand and Mozambique. Greta told her there had never been a school or a church there, and Mavis couldn't get the request out of her mind.

When she wrote to the missionary who had discovered the need, he responded that it was a very difficult place and that he didn't think a woman would survive. Mavis recalls her surprised reaction, "Who is he to tell God who he wants to use there?"

She continued to pray fervently for guidance—and for the means to get there. She finally told the Lord, "If you want me to go, provide the money for the bus fare—and not a penny more."

Within days she received a letter from Greta with five pounds (about $7.50 in 1958), saying that since Mavis wasn't working she'd need money to live on. She didn't know of Mavis's interest to go to Egazini. But that was only half the fare, and Mavis reminded God of her bargain. Four days later another sister, who knew nothing of her plans, sent her a five-pound note. Now she had exactly what she needed for the bus fare to Mseleni, the nearest mission station to Egazini. In faith she packed her things and took the bus to the mission station.

Establishing a School

A few days later, in February 1958, a missionary flew her in the mission plane to the remote area, far from roads or stores. As the plane circled the crude huts below, something in her heart said, "This is where God wants you to be."

She had second thoughts, however, when she saw the round hut made of reeds that was to be her home. The reeds allowed ventilation but no privacy! The dirt floor held nothing but a footlocker, not even a grass mat to sleep on.

One of the three wives of the chief's headman, who was also the witch doctor, came to welcome her and explained what she could expect: "This is my mother-in-law's hut. From time to time she'll visit you, but don't be afraid, she won't hurt you." As Mavis listened she realized the dead mother-in-law returned in the form of a snake.

Deathly afraid of snakes, Mavis told the woman, "When you gave this hut to me you gave it to Jesus. I don't think Jesus and your mother-in-law will get along."

In the weeks ahead in spite of fears and privation, Mavis seemed to float above all the limitations and difficulties of the task God had given her. It mattered not that she didn't receive a cent for her work. She started her school under a spreading indigenous tree. Her twenty-five students ranged in age from three to twenty years of age. When an "ancestral" snake joined her class the students refused to obey her command to kill it, so she learned not to make a fuss over it. In six months most of the children were reading at a second-grade level; mothers were coming after school to learn to read. She started a Sunday service, and even the witch doctor sat on the ground with the others and listened.

Mavis recalls, "I don't remember once feeling, 'I'm starving; why don't people help me?' I was fully content at what the Lord was doing." But the primitive conditions took a toll on her health.

Her diet consisted primarily of peanuts, sweet potatoes, and sugar cane. Her water came from a contaminated stream. She had no money to purchase food, even if there had been a store nearby. Without a latrine of any kind, she feared taking the path into the woods, and her digestive system eventually locked up.

By October she realized she couldn't continue and asked some of the schoolgirls to help her walk to the hospital four hours away. Seeing her emaciated condition, the doctor encouraged her to return to her home in Natal. After she left, the mission sent a replacement teacher; today children meet in a well-built schoolhouse, and the church congregation meets in its own building.

Mavis began to sense the need to attend Bible school and after another year of teaching applied to the Johannesburg Bible Institute (JBI). The school gave her a full scholarship, and she earned her room and board by working for a local missionary family.

An Unexpected Romance

On weekends Mavis helped run a youth club in Soweto, the black township outside Johannesburg proper. Her coworker, Jerry Nkosi, had already graduated from JBI and was seeking to bring Christ to the disenfranchised youth who lived in the bleak and often violent township. As a local boxer he attracted many young people.

Mavis had met Jerry several years earlier when he visited ETTC, and though they had common interests a romantic relationship was farthest from her mind. She didn't even suspect Jerry's intentions when he borrowed the missionary's blue Kombi to take her to the zoo. Even though dating was frowned upon in the African culture she grew up in, Mavis felt freer in the sophistication of Johannesburg.

She recalls their conversation. "Out of the blue Jerry asked me to marry him. No dating, no warning. I laughed and said, 'You know, Jerry, this is very common with Christian young men. They see a Christian girl and think that she is looking for a husband. I told the Lord I'm not going to get married, so just forget it.'"

But Jerry didn't forget it—and he won Mavis's heart. In January 1962, before Mavis began her last year at Bible school, they were married. In spite of their agreement that they would wait until after graduation to start their family, Mavis became pregnant.

"I had my baby in October," she remembers. "I was in the middle of finishing up my term papers. I took all my work to the hospital—in between pains I was writing." She graduated that December, first in her class.

For the next ten years she and Jerry directed an exciting youth ministry called Youth Alive in Soweto. They and their missionary coworkers built a modern youth center in the middle of the township, attracting thousands of young people—the best students and leaders of all the high schools in the area. While society was telling these young people that they were inferior, second class, and had a hopeless future of drudgery and servanthood, Youth Alivers were learning that they were created in the image of God, who loved them and had a wonderful plan for their lives.

While raising her three children Mavis led youth clubs, counseled at retreats, cooked at camps, and kept the ministry financial accounts (bathing the ledgers with tears as she struggled to teach herself accounting). Countless girls came to "Sis May" to pour out their problems and learn how to follow Christ.

The Call to Texas

In 1970 a Youth Alive team of four young men traveled to the U.S., accompanied by the Nkosis. For three months they visited churches and high schools across the country, performing their African traditional music and dance and sharing their testimony of what Christ meant to them. High school principals opened their assemblies, and American young people flocked to hear these young men.

But for Jerry and Mavis this visit brought a shocking revelation. "We observed a lack of ministry to black young people. We visited five camps to learn what would work at home, but we only saw black young people in one, and that was because they were a basketball team."

When Reuben Conner, a black pastor, invited Jerry to come to work with young black people in the inner city of Dallas, the Nkosis prayed seriously about his offer. By now Youth Alive had a good staff of trained leaders to carry on the ministry. And in their hearts they were concerned about the future of their own children in South Africa where apartheid was tightening its noose and discontent was broiling underneath.

In 1973 Jerry and Mavis and their three children, Lena, Hazel, and Howell, moved to Dallas, Texas, to begin working with teens in the low-income housing developments in the city. After their years of experience and the encouraging results at Youth Alive, they fully expected to see a similar response.

But Mavis sadly explains, "We saw a lack of serious commitment to the Lord among the African-American Christians. There's more church than personal commitment. We found it very difficult to disciple people here."

The lack of family structure concerns her deeply. She remembers black young people in the clubs in Dallas asking her children, "Are they *both* your parents—the parents of all three of you?"

Mavis remembers how excited and interested South African girls were about the subject of marriage. "Here," Mavis reports, "marriage is not something common. The girls aren't familiar with or even interested in weddings. When they see a wedding they know the marriage won't last long."

But she understands the reason too. "Girls come from families of just mothers and grandmothers. In the project where we work there are three hundred units. I don't think I'm exaggerating to say it would be a miracle if you had ten families with both husband and wife. Young people don't know what family and love is. Even projecting God as Father presents a problem. 'Father is a man I've never seen, I don't even know. Is God that kind of father?'"

Yet in the face of these problems, the Nkosis persevered. They formed the Urban Action board, raised money, and recruited and trained volunteers to run the clubs. They prayed for the use of a building in the development that was sitting empty and were granted permission to turn it into a clubhouse and offices. As long as funds came in, they took inner-city kids to camp—now they settle for six weeks of day camp at the center.

At the height of the ministry they had eight clubs. Jerry ran the teenage club; with his broad smile and booming voice he seemed to have a magical charm that attracted teenagers. They knew he loved them. He focused on key young people with potential, and today some of them are educated with good jobs.

Carrying the Burden Alone

Just two years after their arrival in the United States, Jerry started having health problems. He had a heart attack and had to have bypass surgery. In 1989 he had a stroke and another in 1990, and though he continued to work in Urban Action, Mavis carried the heavy end of the load. After suffering another heart attack, Jerry knew that he was dying. He was able to have long talks with his children and Mavis, and she promised him that as long as the Lord gave her strength, she would continue the ministry.

But continuing the club ministry, dealing with Lena's problems, and giving Cory and Cameron the love and care they needed became a daunting task. Mavis could see the anger festering in Cory whenever his mother came to pick him up at high school, obviously under the influence of alcohol. Even three-year-old Cameron would stamp his foot and scream, "I'm very angry," when he didn't even know the meaning of anger. Something had to change.

Mavis put Cameron in a day-care center after she asked Lena to leave, since she was still involved in the club ministry. But it pained her to see what was happening to this usually cheerful child. "He was fighting and scratching the kids. We didn't know how to help him," Mavis explained. "We [Hazel and Howell and I] prayed for him, talked with him, gave him all the love we could.

"When he was able to understand I sat down and explained the real problem his mother had with drinking. I explained that it wasn't safe for him to live with her. Little by little he loosened up. He accepted the Lord at the age of four in my Bible club, and now he's very happy to stay with me. In kindergarten he would write notes—'Thank you Grandma for razing me.'"

Mavis admits that she's concerned that the boys have not had a father figure in their lives since Jerry passed away. "Being boys they need and deserve a close contact with a man. Howie, my son, does the best he can to interact with them. One day Cameron said to his cousin, 'Alex, you are very fortunate to have your mom and dad together.'"

Cory, who is now in his early twenties, is completing college and talks about joining Urban Action as a missionary. But Mavis still wonders, "How will living without a man on a daily basis affect how they relate to their wives? They've not been in a situation where they have seen a man taking care of his wife and children."

For several years Lena lost jobs and even a place to live, but Mavis quietly rejoices that Lena has finally responded to rehabilitation and is attending church. Mavis praises God for the turnaround she's seen in her daughter's life. The boys are gradually warming up to their mother when she comes to visit or goes to church with the family. Mavis hopes that eventually Lena will be able to work as an x-ray technician again and that the boys will be able to live with her.

When asked if it will be hard to let them go after the many years she's cared for them she responds, "It won't be hard. I don't want them to be devastated when the Lord takes me. They have been so attached to me. I'd like for them to be with their mother."

Now at seventy-five Mavis continues to care for her two grandsons. Actually she feels having young people in the house has helped her to keep in touch with the children in the housing projects where she serves every week.

"There's such a difference with children today and the children we worked with when we first started," she explains. "Having Cameron helps me; he has taught me things."

She laughs, "Compared to the children in the clubs Cameron is an angel. Today children don't obey adults; they don't mind anybody. They don't fear authority, parents, teachers; they don't fear God. You talk to a kid and he replies, 'What are you going to do about it?'"

Looking for Help

Mavis continues to visit churches to share the opportunities of working with children in the inner city. She tells them, "I'm not asking for your money; I'm asking you to volunteer. Come and teach in the Bible clubs."

But she says the people in the black evangelical churches have told her that they are afraid to go into South Dallas. In one well-to-do megachurch Mavis couldn't keep from speaking out of her passion. "I'm not from here, but I'm in South Dallas until eleven at night. I've never seen anyone being mugged or attacked."

Then she asserted boldly, so out of character from her usual shy and gentle demeanor, "I'll be very frank, because you're black like me. Probably ten or fifteen of you have grandmothers or even mothers who live there. You ought to be ashamed. There are souls there who need to be saved. They are not going to come here to the church."

Because of lack of volunteers only five clubs remain, one of which is for preteen girls. Mavis sees their desperate need. "When they hit thirteen they start having babies. But we don't just teach the Bible; we teach etiquette and hygiene, take them places, and teach them to cook. We teach them how to be women."

Mavis doesn't often hear affirmation from parents, but one mother called to thank her, saying, "I just appreciate what you did for my daughter. She's a lady."

One young volunteer grew up attending Urban Action clubs and day camps. Raised by her grandmother, she came from a depressed situation almost like Cameron's and Cory's. Mavis comments, "I'm encouraged to see one or two really established like her grow up in the Lord, get out of the project, and have a better life.

"What keeps me going? It's the same thing that kept me going at the beginning, the burden for the children. The Bible clubs are the only place where these children have love, let alone hearing about the Lord. There's nothing else out there.

"I'm not sure how long the Lord wants me to continue in the Bible club part of the ministry. I'm tired physically and emotionally. But the burden is still there and the desire to see something going on."

She is encouraged that a young black couple with roots in South Dallas is praying about joining Urban Action. Mavis feels she should hang in there, helping them to get on their feet and introducing them to the people in the project.

"As far as what the Lord wants me to do from now until he calls me home? I know there will be something else. My heart is in this ministry." At this stage only God knows what that "something else" is.

SIX

HOW THE CHURCH HELPS WOMEN FINISH WELL

What I want for the rest of my life is to deal gracefully and graciously with the decrements of aging so that by example and testimony I give others the courage to see that the missions and ministry of the aged are as important as of youth and are important to youth.

Ruth Harriet Jacobs, *Be an Outrageous Older Woman*

Martha taught second grade for thirty-five years. She loved the children, especially their inquisitive minds and transparency. Over the years she earned her M:Ed., which increased her salary and career opportunities. She helped in curriculum planning and in developing her school district's pension plan.

She attended a large vibrant church near her home, though she felt she didn't have time or energy to get seriously involved. But she enjoyed the excellent preaching and the quality programs and teaching it offered and was quite comfortable "taking" its goodness into her life.

As retirement drew close, however, she realized she needed a change. She had never married, but her pension would allow her to live comfortably without financial worries, so she was free to pursue her dreams.

Even before the final day of school, Martha determined that she would get involved in her church. In the past she had received invitations to various senior adult functions, and she knew it was time to quit simply taking and start giving.

Fortunately her church's program for senior adults had a place to use her gifts. She started attending the monthly Friday morning training program with about 150 other seniors. The leaders encouraged them to sit around the table with the same eight people at each meeting. Soon Martha became the leader of her table. These men and women became her "second family," ready to step in to support each other at a moment's notice.

Observing Martha's obvious organizational skills, the pastor of seniors asked her to serve on the leadership team for the senior adults. Martha helped develop training pertaining to their needs and highlighted issues to help them grow. All this was similar to the kind of work she'd done with the school district. On occasions she acted as the MC for the Friday meeting, which she enjoyed since she had led many meetings during her career and felt confident standing in front of an audience.

On alternate Fridays Martha participated in one of the weekly Bible study groups and found herself growing in her Christian walk as never before. Because the classes were interactive instead of "being preached to," she could offer insights from her life as a teacher, while getting her own questions answered.

Martha kept in touch with former colleagues from school and often invited them to a training program or other meeting she knew they would be interested in. At one such meeting they appreciated listening to a geriatric doctor who spoke about prescription medications and dangerous interactions. Hands flew up all over the audience with questions for that doctor! This also opened the door for Martha to share her maturing faith, and she had the joy of helping one of her colleagues take the step of faith in Christ.

Martha had a warm relationship with her widowed father who lived several hundred miles from her. When he died suddenly her tablemates from the Friday morning session rallied around her. One drove her to the town where her father had died. The pastor to seniors, a woman, called her immediately and brought her books to help with the grief process. Later Martha was able to attend a grief workshop sponsored by the church. Even though she had no blood relatives nearby, loving friends surrounded her with care.

The small group prayer time with the leadership team strengthened Martha's prayer life and faith. She began to develop an interest in the world through the prayer requests expressed by others in the group. As she listened to the pastor to seniors make preparations for a mission team to Guatemala, she began praying about whether this should be her next step. Maybe they needed a schoolteacher for a year or two in Guatemala?

What Women Are Finding in the Church

Don't take Martha's experience for granted! She is a composite picture of a woman who has found a satisfying adult ministry in her church, which meets her needs, utilizes her gifts, and gives her opportunities to serve. She represents the longing of many senior women who want to use their spiritual gifts in their churches. More than 80 percent of those who responded to the questionnaire I sent out indicated they wanted to use their gifts in the church.

But while the respondents generally gave a positive evaluation of the opportunities in their churches, only 48 percent agreed that they provided satisfying fellowship with their peers. The responses came from a broad spectrum of churches from mainline denominations, independent, and charismatic churches, but it doesn't seem that either the type or the size of a church affected the response.

Often what they *didn't* say gave the clues as to where women were hurting in their churches. The graph below indicates the percentage of women who did not select a positive response to the question:

My church's program for senior adult women

a. [*does not*] give me opportunity to use my gifts and talents	19 percent
b. [*does not*] makes me feel valued, loved, and affirmed	30 percent
c. [*does not*] provide in-depth mature Bible teaching that relates to my stage in life	50 percent
d. [*does not*] offer me training for various ministry options	67 percent
e. [*does not*] adequately include senior women in decision-making, policy direction, leadership roles	53 percent
f. [*does not*] provide opportunities for outreach and cross-cultural training	43 percent
g. [*does not*] have a strong intercessory prayer group	59 percent

When we broke down the responses by education, 33 percent of those who had not attended college indicated that their church "unintentionally makes me feel unimportant."

In the focus groups I conducted I was able to elicit more in-depth responses from the women. I noted a generally positive reaction to their church (as we'll discuss later). But hurts and disappointments slipped out in their uninhibited discussions with each other. It seems society's attitudes toward senior women have filtered into the church as well. I heard comments such as:

I feel unimportant because the program is geared to single moms.

My church's program is aimed mainly at younger people.

Even when I offer to help I'm not accepted; it seems the younger ones can do things faster.

This attitude was fleshed out in the experience a former mission colleague of mine had. The church she attended had a minimal missions program, but the pastor, to his credit, wanted to hold their first missions conference. He announced that he was forming a committee to plan the conference and invited those who were interested to attend a planning meeting.

My colleague and her husband wanted to contribute from their years of experience overseas and in mission administration. A group of about eight others who were either retired missionaries or serving in home offices of missions attended the meeting. Most were at or beyond retirement age. What a rich reservoir of experience they represented.

One of the church staff led the meeting, and a lively discussion followed with several ideas tossed into the ring. The staff person had come with suggestions as well, but some were unrealistic.

Once the meeting was over, no one who attended ever heard anything more about the committee. Via the grapevine they learned that the pastor was looking for fresh new ideas and feared that old-timers would repeat the same old scenarios they had seen in the past.

What a missed opportunity to utilize the valuable experiences of those who had been there before, while integrating with the ideas of a younger generation!

Youth — Most Important Age Group in the Church?

It's understandable that most churches focus primarily on younger people. After all, isn't this the future of the church? But logically it does not make sense to ignore the fastest growing segment of the population—those over sixty-five. By 2011 the first baby boomer will turn sixty-five and the floodgates of aging adults will pour across our nation. By 2020 there will be as many people over sixty-five as twenty and younger.[1]

God loves seniors as much as he does children. If he didn't love us that much, why would he leave us here so long? Since seniors are generally closer to facing eternity, there is an urgency about giving them the opportunity to receive the gospel and grow in their faith.

For Rosalyn Staples, senior adult pastor at Elmbrook Church in Wisconsin, the most difficult part of working with seniors is the realization that this is their last chance. When she previously worked with children she at least had the consolation that they would have opportunities to hear the truth and respond to it as they moved through life. But for seniors, this is the end of the line!

Yet in spite of this urgent need, and the realization that only 36 percent of seniors who are seventy-five years and older claim to be born again,[2] very few churches have a full-time pastor for seniors or a strong senior outreach program.

Corporate America is beginning to target older people because it pays off on their bottom line, but the church has been slow to take the lead. A study of older adult ministry in the United Methodist Church found that the church hesitates to explore ministry to older adults with any intentionality and diligence. According to author Win Arn, "When one looks for an aggressive outreach program for older adults, it is very difficult to find in the structure of most denominations today."[3]

While this is gradually changing, many are afraid their churches will appear to be dying if they have a large number of old people. One pastor told me that a couple leaving his church remarked to others, "You should leave that church because it's an old folks church."

Ageism in the Church

Ageism is perpetuated in the church when leaders believe that people are less valuable as they age. Win Arn describes some of the possible signs of ageism in his book *Catch the Age Wave:* an unbalanced emphasis on youth without proportionate outreach to older adults; a major part of the budget dedicated to young people in contrast to a proportionate budget assigned to ministry to seniors; selecting a younger pastor over an older more qualified one; under-representation of older people on boards and committees; ignoring the experience and wisdom of older adults in teaching and evangelism roles.[4]

Because we fear aging (and thus avoid dealing with it) or simply because of ignorance, myths about senior adults in the church are commonly accepted. Dr. Janet Peifer lists some of those myths:

1. Having large numbers of older adults in the congregation is a sign of a dying church, something to be lamented and avoided if possible. Outreach must focus on the young.
2. Older church attenders are happiest when their activities and educational classes consist of persons their own age.
3. Persons over seventy years of age have little to offer their congregations because their ideas are outdated and their methods are irrelevant to today's church life.
4. Homebound/frail elderly members have all their needs met by family members and community organizations. The church has more important things to do than function as a social service agency.
5. Most active older adults are interested in a life of leisure and travel and do not care to be involved in committed church or community service.
6. Older adults are set in their ways and cannot adapt to, understand, or accept changes in church, family, and community.
7. Older adults can grow spiritually until afflicted with dementia, then church services, rituals, and spiritual input become meaningless.
8. Most congregations currently offer excellent services and activities for their older adults, so they should just keep up the good work.

9. Old age is synonymous with depression because of loss of role and independence, as well as loss to death of many loved ones.[5]

A common understanding propounds that everyone over sixty-five years of age has the same interests and will happily belong to the same Sunday school class or small group. In fact, age is not the only common denominator. Seniors may be the most heterogeneous group of all, having come from different backgrounds and experiences over many years. With age comes a certain amount of self-confidence to be themselves and not worry about conformity. Teenagers are actually the most homogeneous conformists in society!

It is not unusual to find that young seniors (in their late fifties and sixties) are not interested in joining a senior group made up of people in their seventies and eighties. They don't want to be with those "old people."

While many older people, especially women, live in poverty, seniors are not all poor. Only 10 percent of older people live below the poverty line in this country. Nor are they all in poor health— 70 percent over sixty-five enjoy good to excellent health.

Yet there is enough truth in these myths to have affected our churches, and too many pastors design their senior adult programs around this misinformation. Everyone knows an old person who is unwilling to change or who is a constant complainer. Every pastor has heard a senior refuse to accept responsibility, declaring, "I've done that. It's time for someone else to do it."

But for the few who fall into this category, many more like Martha long to use their gifts. They want to serve in creative ways. Yet too many churches allow these myths to limit their programs to: (1) entertainment for the healthy and (2) care for the frail and sickly. Rather, churches should challenge older people to use their retirement for the glory of God—to "go for it."

In reviewing one church's senior adult program I noticed heavy doses of "lunch, dinner, potluck, buffet, one-day outing with lunch in a restaurant." While fellowship around food can be a valuable part of the church's program—it is far from

God's best design for our extended life span, not to mention the implications for our expanded waistlines.

Are We Propagating the Myths?

As a senior woman I need to check my attitudes so that I do not strengthen these myths into reality. Periodically a self-examination of my own contribution to attitudes of ageism in the church may pull me up short:

Am I resistant to change?

Am I critical of new ideas?

Do I want to be merely entertained?

Do I resist taking any responsibility because I'm lazy?

Am I afraid to give generously for fear I'll be taken advantage of or for lack of trust in God's care?

Do I hang on to a position long after I should have passed the baton?

Am I a complainer or gossip rather than an encourager and pray-er?

Am I unwilling to try anything new?

Do I give in at the first sign of my physical weakness?

Am I involved in a constant "organ recital" (talking about my ailments)?

Am I unwilling to reach out to new people in the church, yet complain that people in the church are unfriendly?

Do I consider children and young people in the church a noisy distraction rather than an opportunity to love and nurture the next generation?

Issues the Church Must Face

Thankfully in the church as a whole interest in ministry and outreach to seniors is growing. As the baby boomers age, they will see to that! More churches are putting pastors for senior adults on their staffs and utilizing trained laypeople to lead senior programs. The Christian Association of Senior Adults Ministries (CASA)[6] brings pastors and lay leaders together to share ideas and train leaders through annual conferences. They also publish a quarterly newsletter. But even as the realization of the increasing senior influence is growing, most churches will have to make a major paradigm shift in their philosophy and programs. Staffs will have to consult with seniors on how to meaningfully meet their needs and utilize their gifts.

Practical Issues

By law all institutions must be handicap accessible, and other facilities and equipment need to be adapted for seniors with limitations. In a church I attended I noticed that older people were singing from words printed in the bulletin even though the words were also projected overhead. I realized this was an accommodation to their vision. Whereas churches have long provided busing for their Sunday school children, more will need to provide some form of transportation for the growing number of frail elderly, especially women, who can no longer drive or who live in retirement communities.

REDISCOVERING GIFTS

When 80 percent of the respondents to my questionnaire said that the church used their gifts, I'm afraid I questioned the validity of the response. My experience working with women for years has been that many women do not know what their spiritual gifts are. They think they are using their gifts when they do whatever they can to help.

Spiritual gifts combine our natural abilities with God-given ones that the Spirit of God anoints to enable us to further His kingdom. Over the years we may have gained experience in counseling, in decision making, in organizing and planning, which God now wants to use in a special way. Some have had opportunities to handle finances in a business that can be used in kingdom building. We may have gone through deep waters in our personal lives, causing us to develop a gift of wisdom or discernment. As we've grown spiritually our pastoral gifts of nurturing and teaching may have emerged gradually like a butterfly out of a cocoon. The church now has the opportunity to harvest these resources and put them to work in the kingdom.

Women will need to be reassured of their worth and encouraged to take risks. Many women have humbly accepted a second-class position in life and feel it presumptuous to step out of their comfortable roles to use the gifts God has been nurturing.

The hundreds of seniors at Elmbrook Church dearly love Pastor Rosalyn Staples, partly because she so openly loves and appreciates them. She goes out of her way to tell them so and assures them she'll be right there beside them as they take new steps in ministry.

Rosalyn has her own idea of how to discover spiritual gifts. "The way you find out what your gift is, you try it. If it works, it's your gift; if not, your friends will tell you," she says. "What I think is the most motivating is to get in over your head. I try to push them a little bit beyond what they can do. There they meet God. They find him picking them up and helping them do it. They're so excited about being able to do what they couldn't do on their own."[7]

Helpful studies about discovering your spiritual gifts go beyond doing simply what your hands find to do. Certainly as we learn about each other's backgrounds and pray together, we can encourage each other to utilize these gifts that can benefit the growth of the kingdom of God.

WHEN CAREER WOMEN RETIRE

The church may be facing the challenging scenario Jean Coyle analyzes in her book. She writes that though baby boomers dropped out of church as teenagers, many are returning as adults. With 72 percent of women working, the concept of gender equality has permeated the culture. Women are looking for programs organized around career concerns, women's issues, lifestyle, and a relationship with God rather than commitment to an institution.[8]

The need for fellowship and friendship can be met at any age level in the church, but an intentional effort should to be made to provide opportunities for friend-making. In response to my questionnaire, the higher the level of education the women had, the less they felt they were able to make close friends in their church. Whether this means that the educated career women are not in the church or that the programs provided don't give them opportunity to find kindred spirits is not clear.

When these career women have retired, what place will they find in our churches? How will their gifts be used, especially gifts of leadership, administration, and teaching? If the church recognizes the valuable resources they will bring to the church, it will need to make room for them.

SINGLE WOMEN'S NEEDS

In the focus groups, I heard the concerns of single women over and over. Ann told of a friend who had no relatives to call on when she had a major health crisis. Fortunately she belonged to a group in the church who cared for her plants and dog and brought her home from the hospital. But what will happen to older single women who don't have such a support group?

"We wake up terrified," says Ann. "There's no one to call. Social isolation occurs early for single women."

This no doubt describes the feelings of many single women —widows, never married, divorced—as they reach their senior years. Single women whose relatives live far away know there's no one to respond to a desperate call in the night. Does the church feel a responsibility for them? The early church was commanded to "care for the widows," and that includes our single sisters.

THINKING CREATIVELY

In order for the church to be ready for retired baby boomers, she ought to be thinking intentionally about new ways to reach them right now. The boomers are forcing a whole new paradigm on the church—even just in sheer numbers. They are healthier, better educated, more widely traveled, and wealthier than their predecessors. And they will want to stay active and utilized far longer. Before boomers arrange to "spend their children's inheritance" pursuing their personal pleasures, the church should be ready with a smorgasbord of opportunities for ministry, training, and service. Just as we've recognized that women should prepare for retirement long before the day actually arrives, so must the church be ready to welcome, train, and utilize the senior boomers, realizing that there is more than one way to "do church."

Dr. John Bristol frequently challenges his Silicon Valley congregation, "It's time to reenlist. When you retire, come to the church the next day to enlist."[9] Dr. Bristol tells his congregation the story of Al Platt, who took early retirement from IBM and has volunteered full-time at the church for the last eleven years in administration. Then John adds, "I don't know how close to retirement you are, but you have to have something to retire to. This might be the greatest opportunity for ministry you've got." John believes that he must reiterate this value over and over until it becomes part of his people's thinking.

EVANGELISM OUTREACH TO SENIORS

It's a known fact that most conversions occur before the age of fifteen, and that by the time a person reaches sixty-five the likelihood that she or he will make a commitment to Christ diminishes drastically. Many senior adults in America have had contacts with the church in their childhood or youth, and Barna's research indicates that 47 percent attend church on any given Sunday. While senior adults are members of churches more than of any other kind of organization, Barna found that 64 percent of seniors do not claim to have a born-again experience.[10]

Does the average church make a serious effort to evangelize seniors? Admittedly it's not easy. Senior adults who have had "bad experiences" in a church resist what they interpret as hypocrisy. Others have never found a vibrant, challenging community of believers to identify with. While 70 percent of seniors claim that their faith is very important to them, apathy, cynicism, and little "walking the talk" permeate the senior culture.[11]

Yet in this climate older people are undergoing some of the most traumatic changes of their lives—death of a spouse, retirement, major physical problems, entering a nursing home, catastrophic medical bills. And studies have shown that these changes often bring a spiritual openness and a willingness to listen to and explore God's truths.

While some churches *are* thinking creatively about how to evangelize senior adults, of the senior adult leaders I interviewed, only two had intentional evangelistic outreaches to them. One church encouraged seniors to invite friends and neighbors to a monthly educational tea where attendees were given literature and were introduced to the gospel. One group who regularly shared the plan of salvation in nursing homes had the thrill of leading a one-hundred-year-old woman to the Lord. They watched her change from a crotchety complainer to a woman of praise.

Another church began a home visitation program to share their faith in their predominantly senior community. Intergenerational teams worked together and encouraged people to attend Sunday school classes. Senior adults who were not able to go on the visitation joined prayer groups and provided meals for the teams.

Intergenerational Opportunities

Of all the dreams and plans for retirement mentioned by women both in answer to my questionnaire and discussion in the focus groups, the desire to mentor younger women in the church had the highest response. Women have a clear awareness that their years of experience—the disappointments and victories—have value and would help younger women. One woman warned, however, that a mentor should not expect to give advice without being asked. "Our big responsibility is to simply be a friend and to pray for them. From that may come some mentoring relationships," she said.

This desire to mentor indicates that senior women want to be part of the whole church and not just mingle with their own age group. If natural opportunities are available to get to know each other across the generations we can learn from each other. One church, which has a strong age-oriented Sunday school hour, offers short-term classes midweek in many subjects taught by staff and qualified lay leaders. I would have had a hard time choosing between "Beginning Greek" and a study of Tolkien's *Two Towers*. You can imagine that the latter attracted a broad spectrum of interested teens, literature majors at local colleges, and seniors who were avid readers of Tolkien.

Intergenerational programs are fraught with difficulty, however. One sixty-four-year-old focus group participant shared her experience as she attended a high school age Sunday school class every week. Her desire was to serve as a listening ear, a counselor, and a pray-er. "We have so much to share," she said, "but the culture is a shield between us. They are respectful and good kids, but it's very challenging with this old face and gray hair to invite them in to my passion for Christ. There have only been a few kids I could pray with." Yet, her attempts may be like seed in young hearts, waiting to sprout into new life at a later date.

With the changing contemporary scene, is division the only answer?

Dr. Greg Waybright, president of Trinity International University, who pastored a church made up of primarily senior adults and college students, doesn't think so. He says,

I am still convinced that the church is the one place in our divided world in which intergenerational ministry and community can be developed. When it happens the rest of the world can look on and see that God must be at work. As Jesus said, "By this shall all men know that you are my disciples: if you have love one for the other." This love is one that must cut across those walls that normally divide human beings, including that of age. The hope that we have in the church is that we have a unity of faith in Jesus Christ—thus being fellow recipients of the Spirit of God. We share a common vision and mission related to evangelism and missions. We have shared values that flow from the preaching and teaching of God's Word. Thus, I am convinced that the church is the one place in the world in which diverse people should be able to experience community with one another and live and serve in unity.[12]

Wonderful as Waybright's model seems, it does not always square with the reality of the growing process churches experience. Other churches have found new unity by creating different kinds of services where people can worship in ways that fit their personal tastes and reflect their backgrounds.

A church I visited in a predominantly senior community had successfully developed a thriving youth program by hiring a vibrant young staff person and building a gym. But they had come to an impasse. On Sunday mornings the drums and synthesizer lay silent as the congregation sang the old gospel hymns to organ and piano accompaniment. In spite of the active youth program, not many young people showed up for church. They had faced the great challenge to intergenerational ministry: music. The church's solution? To hold two services on Sunday evenings, one contemporary and the other traditional. They hope the spirit of unity will continue in spite of this separation.

How Do Senior Women Know They Are Valued?

George Barna's research validates the importance of the role of women in the church. He reports, "Without women, Christianity would have nearly 60 percent fewer adherents. Women shoulder most of the responsibility for the health and vitality of the Christian faith in the country." Women are 33 percent more likely than men to volunteer in a church; 29 percent more likely than men to attend church and to share their faith with others, and 23 percent more likely to donate to a church.[13]

The pastors I've interviewed have been very positive and affirming about the value of older women in the church—even the ones who don't use the women's organizational or leadership skills. One pastor declared, "If it weren't for women, you wouldn't have a church. They are the pray-ers, and are more sensitive to the needs of people than men; but women are not in the loop of problem solving. Problems are directed to the leadership of the church." Thus in his church he would not turn to a "wise woman" for counsel about a relational problem with a woman parishioner.

Senior women know they are valued by the senior pastor's attitude toward them. He or she does not patronize them. Personal concern for their needs is helpful, but more important is a willingness to utilize their gifts and to include them in the ministry. It may help if the pastor is also a senior, but that need not necessarily be true. The most loving pastor toward seniors I've met was in his late forties.

Senior women know they are valued when they are included in leadership, asked to be on committees, and are offered training so that they can better serve. The church I attend attracts many seniors who are represented on all the boards and committees of the church, along with the boomers and young people.

Senior women know they are valued when the church provides a staff member, either paid or volunteer, to focus on their needs and to plan their programs. Since women outnumber men in the church and far outnumber them as they reach their seventies and eighties, it makes sense that that staff person is a woman. Women feel a woman will understand their needs and problems better than a man.

Senior women know they are valued when their pastor to seniors promotes a vibrant, exciting program that stretches their minds and hearts rather than simply providing food and entertainment. One of the most challenging programs I ran into in my research was a visitation program to "hard-to-visit" people. An insightful city welfare department invited a local church to assign senior volunteers to visit people no one else wanted to visit—the alcoholics and drug-addicted homeless for whom they'd found shelter but no solutions to their lives.

During the first year fifteen senior men and women adopted these difficult cases and visited them every week. One woman met for almost a year with an alcoholic who had cirrhosis of the liver. She shared Christ with him as she sat by his bed in his smoke-filled room, but she doesn't know what his response was. At the end he asked that she be with him when he died, since he had no one else. This retired secretary says, "It's the first time I saw someone die, but I wouldn't have missed that for the world."

This church provides a seniors' program with training, Bible studies, fish fries, and fun—but the seniors involved in this difficult ministry know that God still has challenges for them with which their church is willing to trust them.

Senior women know they are valued when they are offered programs of excellence and Bible teachers who understand and speak to their issues. Programs that attract people of all backgrounds and educational levels provide a resource for friend making—one of the greatest needs as seniors age and lose spouses and old friends.

Senior women know they are valued when the church attempts to take their musical tastes into consideration in the worship of the church. Without question, the resolution of the music problem requires give and take from all age levels, but a church that includes traditional hymns along with modern worship gives everyone an opportunity to worship—and to learn to adapt to one another's needs.

Senior women know they are valued when the church helps them to live out their retirement years meaningfully, finishing well the race set before them.

The following model of finishing well, Win Couchman, is such a woman.

Win Couchman

A WISE WOMAN

> The Old Testament speaks of wise women to whom leaders, kings, and prophets turned for advice and counsel. Where are the "wise women" in our churches today to whom leadership can look for spiritual direction and help? Win Couchman has demonstrated what such a woman can mean in the church.

Win and Bob had hoped this day would never come. They waited all day in the hospital room together with their grown children. Win had come in that morning for an angiogram to test her heart function, but delay followed delay. By afternoon they were bored and tired of figuring out the gadgets and tubes in the room. They bantered back and forth, trying to hide their apprehension over the meaning of the ominous symptoms that had brought Win here.

For some time Win had noted a strange feeling across her back and shoulders and a sense of impending death whenever she went for a walk—which she did regularly. The first visit to a cardiologist indicated "nothing serious," but when the discomfort continued the doctor scheduled Win for an angiogram.

To Win, who'd had confidence in God's care and provision since her childhood, the prospects did not generate fear as much as disbelief. The timing seemed all wrong. Just four and half years before, she and Bob had finally been able to join an international mission, and they were relishing the experience to serve with teams of younger missionaries all over the world. They'd fulfilled the dreams they had to do something meaningful together after Bob's retirement.

Win wrote in her memoirs, "In our early fifties, we began to inquire of the Lord what he wanted us to do and to be in our later years. When should Bob, an engineer, retire? What ought he retire to? What sort of ministry could involve both of us?"[14]

They had both had an interest in missions, especially since they'd become a part of Elmbrook Church in Wisconsin, where their pastor, Stuart Briscoe, lived and breathed a passion for the world. They took a short-term mission trip to Guatemala and came back fired up with excitement. Seeing their enthusiasm, Stuart encouraged them to "blue-sky" it. He counseled, "You two are the Lord's. You aren't kids and you aren't rebels. You want to please Him, and He knows that. He isn't a monster. He has been shaping your desires for years, and He loves you. . . . Think of what you would love to do and expect your heart's desire to be one indication of His will for you."[15]

At a missions conference some months later Win felt a compelling desire to respond to the speaker's challenge to offer herself for overseas service. She wondered what Bob was thinking. Tentatively she reached for his hand, and as their eyes met, they both stood up as though the Spirit had pushed the same button.

In their mid-sixties, after Bob's retirement, they fulfilled a long-term commitment designed just for them in many places of the world. They worked in Australia, the Philippines, Austria, and Eastern Europe. It's understandable that Win wondered how the news this day would impact their future.

After the catherization the doctor returned with the result—good and bad. Her heart had not been damaged, but several arteries were clogged. His advice—go on medications, reduce the stress level of three moves a year, which their assignment required, and consider staying near quality medical facilities should an emergency arise. Heavyhearted, Win walked out of the doctor's office with the painful realization, "I am no longer a missionary."

But her family thanked God that she wasn't in serious danger; her church welcomed her back with open arms. One of the pastors said to her, "You've just been reassigned to Jerusalem."

Rooted in the Word of God

Win and Bob had served in their "Jerusalem" for many years, and God allowed them to have experiences that prepared them well. Trials that develop character filled their first years of marriage.

They both testify that it was "love at first sight" when they were seventeen. In fact, Win can describe what she was wearing and where she was sitting when she first laid eyes on Bob. Bob's father owned the town newspaper. "So Bob thought he was really hot stuff—but he was unspeakably gorgeous," she remembers. They met in the high school study hall one morning, and the sparks that ignited have lasted a lifetime.

Right after graduation Bob was drafted into the military early in World War II. When his ship lost its bow and returned to port for two weeks, Win and Bob were married before he left for another fourteen months at sea.

She recalls her almost naïve struggle with God for Bob's safety. "I thought, if I don't get this settled with God I hope he'll just kill me. I know Bob won't come back. He'll die and if I'm not sure I'll be right with God I'll have nothing. I thought, how can I bargain with him? I'll quit wearing lipstick and reading magazines; that's all I knew to do. Wasn't he nice to give me peace on the basis of such foolishness?"

Bob *did* return safely from the war and from another stint in the Korean War. Five children arrived but the fifth died at birth—something Win keeps hidden in her heart—before the family moved from California to Wisconsin.

During these years Win steeped herself in the Scriptures; she loved to study the Bible every day while Bob was at work and the children were in school. She recalls the vital change that took place in her life as a result of these studies. "In my early thirties, during a long personal study of the book of Romans, I finally understood that the Holy Spirit was the live-in God for all believers, that he had the power I had lacked to live right. I saw that he would direct any part of my life that I asked him to. This was the ingredient that had been missing in my comprehension of Christianity."[16] Her legalistic foolishness had changed to living faith.

Responding to a Need

Bringing up teenagers in the sixties tested Christian parents to the limit. The counter-revolution influenced everything from entertainment to personal mores, and the churches generally were not prepared to deal with the issues. As Win and Bob feared the influence on their own children they felt they needed to take action. So they opened their home to high school students for Bible study and open discussion on how the Word of God spoke to the issues the teens were facing. From a small beginning of a few teens, Forever Family, as it was soon called, grew until their little house was bursting at the seams several nights a week.

Shortly after the Couchmans started Forever Family, Stuart Briscoe accepted the call to pastor the small but growing Elmbrook church and moved to Wisconsin from England. He and his wife, Jill, had worked with unconventional kids there and hoped to be able to continue such a ministry through the church.

Stuart recalls, "My first encounter with Win was on a visit to Elmbrook in the late sixties. I was invited to meet a group of young people. I went to the address given to me and found the road leading to it blocked with numerous cars, all of the 'rust bucket' design. It was bitterly cold and snowing, bleak and inhospitable—just normal Wisconsin winter weather. On arriving at the driveway to the house I was surprised to find stacks of furniture standing in the snow. In response to my knocks on the door the person inside tried to open the front door but was at first unable to do so because of the literally wall-to-wall kids who had taken the space vacated by the furniture stacked in the snow."

For thirteen years Win and Bob opened their home to young people, moving the furniture out of the house to make room for them. Many came out of the drug culture or were caught in the grip of alcoholism and confused by the sexual mores around them. But they learned that they could ask questions without condemnation and found in Win and Bob not only mentors but friends. Today many of those young people have established strong Christian families and are living in obedience to the Word of God.

With the growing opportunities at Elmbrook Church and the friendship that had developed between the Couchmans and the Briscoes, Win found herself filling many niches in the church. She taught eighth graders in Sunday school, wrote camp curriculum and small group leaders' manuals, and spoke at women's meetings and conferences across the country. She and Bob taught marriage seminars.

As her influence spread, many turned to her intuitive gift of counseling. Though she never attended college, Win followed the model of her own mother who "mentored" others, long before the word was popular. Win's mother taught a Sunday school class of prisoners well into her eighties. She in turn had seen her own mother model a godly life of faith and prayer.

Win writes in her memoirs, "On my last visit home when she was still alive, Grandmother was past ninety and bedridden. I asked her what she thought about heaven. . . . Finally she said, a trifle disdainfully, as though I had asked something frivolous, 'Oh, honey, I really have not thought much about heaven. There is so much here to think and pray about.'"

Win comments, "Her pattern of prayer gave me the realization, early on, that a sick, old woman could still be fully engaged in ministry."[17]

Noah's Nudge

As the Couchmans neared sixty, Win felt that they should be thinking about getting out of youth work. In her times of prayer she asked God what his will was for them, and he seemed to be saying, "Noah." She read the story over and over, looking for some clue to God's guidance. And then it struck her. God saved a few people in the protected structure of the ark as long as they needed it. Win explains, "But then they had to get out before they got smelly from living in those close quarters!"

She saw the clear analogy. When they had started Forever Family few programs existed to meet the needs of young people. But by the early eighties youth ministries that had their pulse on the youth culture were popping up all over. Win felt their work had become superfluous and that they should move on.

It was just about this time that they responded to the call of missions at their church and by 1985 had joined International Teams (IT). The director of the mission designed a program specifically for the Couchmans' gifts and abilities. He wisely recommended that they not sell their home, nor consider a lengthy educational program but take advantage of their vast experience in ministry. He arranged for them to live with a team on the IT campus in the States for several months and then go overseas to follow up the teams. Bob would use his engineering skills in various ways and even go behind the Iron Curtain on secret courier work. Win would fill in with teaching and counseling as the needs arose. They expected to live at home for about a third of each year.

Win and Bob danced for joy as they saw God's hand on the plan that seemed to fit their gifts so perfectly. The church family generously pledged so much for their support that they turned some of the money back. The hardest thing was to leave their three grandchildren who lived nearby and especially daughter Liz, who was expecting her first child.

A Time of Testing

The first year brought marvelous new experiences, and Win and Bob felt like children discovering a toy store. They relished the novel experiences they shared with their dedicated team members. Win recalls standing on the garbage dump in Manila, foul smells and humid heat rising around them, as they joined hands to sing Christmas carols led by a young dump dweller and his guitar. A cathedral couldn't have resonated with more glorious praise.

They discovered Europe together when they were based in Austria following up the teams going behind the Iron Curtain. But they found that change also tested their own relationship— each reacted differently to the strange sensations of culture shock. They worked through these tensions, discovering the causes and how to avoid them in the future.

With his engineering and practical skills, Bob was in constant demand. Often gone all day on assignments, he focused on learning computer skills at night. On the other hand, Win felt out of place. She determined not to foist her counseling on team members unless they asked. Some did but not enough to keep her busy. She tended their small apartment, faced the embarrassment of shopping without necessary language skills, and offered to baby-sit for team members. In the training programs in the U.S. she taught Bible classes and about team relationships, but once the teams were involved overseas, they were too busy to study together.

"I couldn't figure out if I'd been any use at all as a missionary," she states regretfully. "I asked God, 'Does this make any sense to you? I feel so utterly useless.'" But she knew that God had called her and Bob, and she believed he had something profitable in mind for them both—at least until they couldn't lug their luggage anymore.

Now at sixty-seven the fateful decision had been made for them. Win's health would not allow her to continue the stressful schedule. She knew her "reassignment to Jerusalem" was from God, and she claimed his words to Joshua for herself:

"You are very old, and there are still very large areas of land to be taken over" (Josh. 13:1).

New Responsibilities

The church joyfully welcomed the Couchmans back. It seemed everyone understood they had no other choice. One day Stuart asked Win and Bob for lunch, and Win was sure he had a new project for her to embark on. Instead he wanted to assure her that it was okay to say no if anyone put pressure on her to take on responsibilities for which she was not ready.

Win soon found her level of comfort and began her volunteer counseling program once again. She gradually accepted speaking and teaching responsibilities, and she and Bob occasionally traveled overseas to speak at short conferences. She also began writing a regular letter to missionaries as part of the church's newsletter. Many missionaries responded to thank her, saying that now they knew she understood what they were going through. Gradually Win recognized that her missionary experience was not a loss; it simply enabled her to be of more help in "Jerusalem."

It was Stuart himself who called on her to consider accepting a new and far-reaching responsibility. For some time he had been encouraging the leaders of the church to study and pray about the role of women in ministry with the hopes that they would adjust the church constitution to allow women elders. However, when they voted, the proposal passed by a very small margin—not a large enough majority for such a drastic change in church polity.

Instead the elders came up with a creative idea. They decided to invite two mature "wise" women who were well thought of and who had used their gifts to build up the body of Christ. They asked these women to sit in on all the elders' meetings and to share their opinions and reservations on every issue—but they would not have a vote. Win was one of the two women.

It would have been hard for her to refuse their warm invitation. They told Win, "If you come, you'll see twelve shining faces, because we need you so badly." Win found these men of God sensitive and willing to listen to any suggestions she made. She feels that her primary role has been to encourage them in prayer.

Even with the increasing responsibilities at the church that had now grown to over five thousand members, Win made time to counsel people, often as many as three two-hour sessions a day.

A woman pastor of senior adults says, "I'm not the only pastor at Elmbrook that considers Win their pastor. If I need to confess or talk about what can't be talked about anywhere else, I go to her. I don't think there are many important issues that I don't take to her to pray about."

Another Roadblock

In the midst of this fruitful "Jerusalem" ministry, Win's heart continued to cause concern. Medications worked for a while, but eventually she had to have an angioplasty—then two, then three.

By 2001 Win had had seven catheterizations and several stents. But no matter what the doctors did, her arteries continued to plug up.

When she was once again in the hospital, Win's Christian cardiologist came to sit beside her bed to discuss the latest failure. Almost apologetically he explained that the only solution was surgery. He had tried everything else to no avail. She needed a quadruple bypass.

Even in this experience, Win learned new things about God. "Adoration has really helped me heal. By the time I had finished my adoration of him, my pain wasn't my focus."

In one way she believes the surgery was a gift from God. "People always expected me to be available to do everything.

God had to do something so big that people would really finally get it that I couldn't do everything."

In her eightieth year, less than a year after surgery, Win felt that she had been fully restored to health—as fully as she could expect. "Being well and being twenty are two different things," she comments dryly. She experienced the expected changes that come with aging—lack of energy, remembering to take medications, sleeplessness. While Win complained of having to write down every appointment in her date book, "leaving nothing to my fickle brain," her colleagues and friends still admired her sharp mind and knowledge of Scripture.

Many of her friends have lost their spouses. Win says if she allowed herself to think about how she would miss Bob—his presence, his listening ear—she realizes how much she would have to learn to do alone. When women ask her if they are too dependent on their husbands, she wonders the same thing. In her memoirs she wrote, "I can only tell the women what I ask myself: 'What would you need to know and need to be able to do, that you don't now know, if your husband died?'"[18]

What Makes a Wise Woman?

Paul lists wisdom as one of the spiritual gifts (1 Cor. 12:8). Just as evangelism is a spiritual gift (Eph. 4:11), which is also required of every believer when the Holy Spirit directs, so we should all seek wisdom. In Christ, the Living Word, "are hidden all the treasures of wisdom and knowledge" (Col. 2:3).

As a young mother, Win immersed herself in the Word. When the Holy Spirit revealed his power and effect upon her life through the study of Romans, she immediately applied these truths.

"I remember that for months after this understanding came to me," she wrote, "I began each day in a private ceremony of restating my commitment to God. I did this gladly and without coercion. It was a glory. From then on, I really wanted Him to direct me."[19]

During her long convalescence after surgery she realized that God was directing her into a new phase of ministry. She had to cut down her counseling hours and for a long time saw people for only fifteen minutes, but this gave her more time to reflect, to think through what she should say, more time to pray.

She had a greater awareness of heaven but also a deeper longing to speak words of comfort and encouragement to those who came for help. She wanted to do as Paul did, to "continue with all of you for your progress and joy in the faith" (Phil. 1:25).

Win would be the last person to describe herself as a wise woman, but her pastor, Stuart Briscoe, thinks otherwise about the Couchmans:

> They model marriage . . . a solid, loving partnership. . . .
>
> They model maturity . . . the genuine maturity of years and spirit that is dynamic and changing, growing and always moving upward. . . .
>
> They model ministry. Scarcely a week goes by without someone sharing what the Couchmans did for them. A fragile homosexual, a distraught mother, a pregnant teenager, a deserted husband. . . . Their ears are open to hear problems, but their mouths are closed.
>
> If the church is something that we are rather than somewhere that we go, then the church is the Wins and Bobs of this world who, when fed with the Word, burn up the calories of truth, and in the energy thus generated see the power of the Spirit released in holy living, corporate commitment, evangelistic zeal, missionary endeavor, and a host of good works. Blessed is the pastor of such a church.[20]

SEVEN

FINDING THE KEY TO FRUITFUL BONUS YEARS

The secret in the search for meaning is to find your passion and pursue it.

Gail Sheehy

Over the years Barbara Hudson pled with the Lord to use her, but at eighty-one years she told him, "Life is over; I'm old and worn out." She didn't know that God was getting ready to use her in a very special way.

Barbara had been involved in drama all her life. She helped with the production of Billy Graham films and wrote plays and trained church drama teams. But she never felt that her life was making a difference. In her late sixties she wrote a series of monologues on women in the Bible from the perspective of looking back on their lives. She performed these monologues in many churches. Now she had received an invitation to prepare dramatic presentations at Hilton Head Island for two-and-a-half million summer visitors.

When she met with the church staff to discuss this possibility she asked, "Do you realize that I'm eighty years old?"

They agreed to a three-month trial. All along her five-day drive to the island she kept asking, "Why me, Lord? Why am I doing this?" Suddenly the Lord made it clear to her. "I'm eighty years old and am the perfect one to present the claims of Christ to all the other seniors who have gone all the way through their lives and careers ignoring Him."[1]

In Ted Engstrom's book *Add Life to Your Years,* Chuck Colson describes what might be termed "golf-course" retirement, the inconsequentiality of a life focused only on personal pleasure and fun.[2] Make no mistake, fun and games have their place in life, especially after we are released from the routine pressures of a job; but those pleasures are not enough to give the Christian life meaning and purpose.

Retirement or release from major responsibilities can present an enticing opportunity to start over again. Or if we are filled with guilt or disappointment that we haven't done more with our lives, we can make the remaining twenty or even thirty years meaningful.

But in spite of the golden promises of a long and more healthy fourth quarter and all the positive aspects of aging we've discussed, starting over at sixty-five is very different from starting out at twenty-five!

Carl Jung warned that when we embark upon new opportunities in the later years of life, "we cannot live the afternoon of life according to the program of life's morning; for what in the morning of life was true will at evening have become a lie."[3]

Our idyllic picture of relaxation, freedom from responsibilities, and time to do whatever we want soon grows old. I overheard a woman in a Florida mobile home park call out across the street to a neighbor, "I'm going to paint the driveway. I'm so bored." Sunny skies, balmy breezes, casual walks around the park, early bird dinners at the restaurant, and lots of time on her hands could not satisfy her longing for meaning.

What Next?

Having reached the long-awaited and/or dreaded point of retirement, and having been crowned as "senior" with all its benefits and disadvantages, where do we go now? While most of us have strength and health to be able to enjoy the second half of our lives with vigor, we need to be realistic about the challenges ahead.

As we've already observed, widowhood adds to the stress of retirement. Besides the trauma of loss and loneliness, many widows face financial difficulties. Women make up three-quarters of the elderly poor, with 12 percent of older women living in poverty.[4] Physical strength eventually deteriorates when illness or disability sets in. These are some of the negative realities of the bonus years that will require courage and praise if they are to be meaningful.

Probably the greatest challenge after retirement is to find new ways to use our gifts and to feel valued, particularly when society stigmatizes older women as incapable or slow. We may have been brainwashed into actually believing it.

But we have learned that fruitful engagement is a key to successful aging and it lowers the rate of depression. More and more adults are working well into their senior years—some out of necessity and many simply because they want to stay active and productive.

A *60 Minutes* report introduced an eighty-three-year-old administrative assistant who had just learned to use the computer and a ninety-year-old machinist who says she will continue to work as long as she can climb the stairs to the shop. "I would be bored to death doing nothing."[5]

If we have developed new interests and skills, maintained a positive attitude, cared for our health, reached out to others, and taken advantage of new learning opportunities, we can be confident God will enable us to do whatever he now expects of us.

We can dream of starting a new ministry, writing a book, teaching women overseas, becoming a counselor, feeding the homeless, mentoring younger women, traveling. Retirement should give opportunity to explore the dreams you had in your youth, the things, you've always wished you could do but never had the time or the resources.

This is the time to try out the latent gifts you've always wanted to use and to let the Holy Spirit nudge you off that plateau you've been stuck on.

However, you may be disappointed in the direction your life has taken; you may even wonder about its purpose. Education may have eluded you—either because of poor choices in youth or financial obstacles. Perhaps your marriage failed or at best proved an exercise in endurance. Maybe your children have disappointed you or are not following God's plan for them. Perhaps you would never call the jobs you held a "career"—they were so mundane and boring. You may have lost a job because of age, which accounts for the fastest growing number of discrimination cases in the nation.

Certainly Jimmy and Rosalynn Carter, former president and first lady of our nation, faced a desperate disappointment when they lost reelection in 1980. Many considered his presidency a failure. Yet Mr. Carter has become one of the most highly respected former presidents in history, using his wisdom and experience around the world to help other countries work through their problems. In a recent poll Carter was listed as the top role model for seniors. He and Rosalynn put Habitat for Humanity on the map as they soiled their hands and risked aching backs working on new homes for the poor.

Jimmy Carter knows what it means to start over. In his book *Everything to Gain* he wrote:

> No matter how much or how little we have accomplished in the first part of our lives, it is never too late for unprecedented experiences. The second half of our lives can actually be a time of greater risk taking for those of us whose responsibilities may have left little room for taking chances before—not foolish or pointless risks, but risks that offer the hope of both real adventure and real reward for ourselves and others. . . .
>
> We have lost some of our youthful self-consciousness. We have been laughed at before and survived. We have been hurt, lonely, disappointed, defeated before and survived. There is no

longer any danger that we will be cut off a promising career before it has begun . . . but we have the added pressure of time.[6]

Volunteering Becomes Second Nature

Indeed there is much to be done, and President George W. Bush has commended Americans for their volunteerism and community service. Half of all people over fifty-five volunteer their services, and the number is growing as baby boomers enter their retirement years. With more money and time on their hands, plus the skills and experiences developed over the years, seniors can contribute to every phase of society and the church. Volunteering can involve hard work and dedication, but it gives purpose and fulfillment to life.

Sometimes doors stand open right in front of our faces, obvious, just waiting for someone to step in. Churches generally have more opportunities than they can fill. The downtown church I attend needs volunteers at a local soup kitchen, in a head-start program for children from low-income families, and at an ecumenical center that provides food, clothing, job search assistance, and medical advice, just to name a few of the community needs, say nothing of ministry needs within the church.

Occasionally it may be difficult to find a place that will utilize our skills and experience and fit our situation perfectly. A psychologist offered himself to several organizations including the Red Cross after 9/11 but never heard from them. No doubt the confusion of the terrible tragedy was to blame. But it may take persistence to follow up inquiries to find the right fit for us.

VOLUNTEERMATCH posts local service opportunities both secular and faith-based on its web site. It has the largest database of volunteer opportunities on the Web. The National Senior Service Corps, a publicly and privately funded entity that works with faith-based groups, schools, and civic organizations, lists countless volunteer opportunities. The Senior Service Corps includes the Retired and Senior Volunteer Program, a Foster Grandparent Program, and the Senior Companion Program. The Christian Association for Primetimers (CAP) provides a personalized profile, comparing skills and interests with their database of over eight thousand organizations worldwide. See appendix A for contact information for these programs.

A Time to Take Risks?

This may be the time to "open the throttle" and take risks—to follow through with an idea or dream you've never acted upon before. Don't give in to the temptation to pull back into a cocoon of safety—to do things the way you've always done them. Sociologist William Sadler found in his studies of the elderly that while 40 percent adapted to change and functioned well, fewer than 10 percent generated self-actualization after age fifty-five.[7] Think of the fun you are missing!

Sixty-eight-year-old pilot Nancy El-Hajj flies the *SeaWind,* a plane built by her husband to be used as a Christian witness at air shows. Nancy has been a professional pilot since she was twenty-five, but after she became a Christian at age fifty-two, she wanted to use her skills and experience for the kingdom. She and her husband designed the plane, which they completed in 2000. The couple travels around the country to air shows, answering questions of people who see the cross, dove, and "Glory Hallelujah" on the wing tips.[8]

Nancy is willing to risk danger to share her faith in a unique manner. We need not look for a bold or risky venture as she did, but we can each do something that will add a new dimension of meaning to our lives. Be willing to take a "small risk"—like taking a plate of cookies to the neighbor you haven't met.

I'm convinced when our purpose is to glorify God, obeying him is not a risk, even when we fail. If he has called us into a particular ministry or activity, he honors our sincere efforts.

Going back to school after sixty-five may seem like a major risk. But the education landscape has changed since I earned my master's degree at fifty. Then a senior was a rarity in the classroom, but today older adults are filling our colleges and universities.

Anne Martindell, former U.S. ambassador to New Zealand and New Jersey state senator, completed her college degree in 2002 at age eighty-seven. Seventy years before, her father had forced her to drop out of college, fearing that she'd become too educated to find a husband. Now she was able to return to finish her degree. She declares that the intellectual stimulation took twenty years off her life, and she's even toying with the idea of graduate school.

Retirement "to" something is vital to keep life from running down. Whether it's taking classes, turning a hobby into a business, or investigating a new career, this could be a turning point in your life.

Again Jimmy Carter has sound advice:

> If we have not achieved our early dreams, we must either find new ones or see what we can salvage from the old. If we have accomplished what we set out to do in our youth, then we need not weep like Alexander the Great that we have no more worlds to conquer. There is clearly much left to be done, and whatever else we are going to do, we had better get on with it.[9]

Passing It On

The women I've met as I've been researching for this book are getting on with it! That's why I've included models of women who are finishing well, so that you can see that there are various ways to do this. It was actually difficult to select these models, for many other women I've met also intentionally seek to capitalize on living the bonus years to the hilt.

In the questionnaire I sent out, several hundred women responded to this question—"What specific ministry/service do you think God expects of you during the years after retirement?" What a variety of ministries, dreams, and plans emerged. (See appendix B for a full list.) The five highest-ranking responses were:

1. Prayer
2. Missions
3. Teaching a Bible study, discipling
4. Mentoring younger women
5. Grandparenting

The *Century Dictionary* defines a mentor as "one who acts as a wise and faithful guide, especially for a younger person; an intimate friend who is also a wise counselor." A buzzword today, *mentoring* goes as far back as the Bible. Barnabas mentored Paul as a young Christian; Moses mentored Joshua to become his successor; Naomi mentored Ruth in the traditional practices of Jewish women.

While many women look forward to mentoring a younger woman, young moms, their grandchildren, or their neighbors, they often do not know how to go about it. Mentoring does not consist of giving unasked-for advice or interfering in the private lives of the mentorees. Rather, as women told me, "Wait for the Lord to open doors, just make friends, and be willing to listen." Often we may be mentoring younger women without even knowing we're doing it. As we befriend them, they watch our lives and learn from our experiences.

Unfortunately the young women who want someone to mentor them may have a difficult time finding mentors. A seminary student says that every woman on her campus is looking for an older woman to mentor her. Cavin Harper, president of Lifequest,[10] seeks to connect senior mentors with college students who, he says, are "standing in line to be mentored."

Many young people today come from dysfunctional homes or have had no grandparents in their lives. They would like a relationship with older people, valuing their wisdom and experience. But Harper says it is hard to find adults who will make such a commitment. Older people often tell him that they have not accomplished anything and have nothing to offer.

One of the best places to bring about these mentoring connections is through the local church. Cross-generational learning used to take place in the home or the Sunday school before age-segregated classes. Putting the generations together in a study group or a work project can prove to be a daunting challenge but worth the effort when bonding takes place.

Today many grannies in America are raising grandchildren, either because the children's parents are divorced or are working and unable to do so. It's estimated that 15 percent of grandparents provide some day care for their grandchildren.

My friend Dot has taken care of her granddaughter since infancy during the day while the child's parents are at work. She didn't want her to be raised by child-care professionals. She admits it's tiring and ties her down, but when she tells stories of the things her granddaughter says and does, she sounds twenty years younger than her seventy-eight years.

All of us with grandchildren should look for ways to do special things with them and to show them the world through our eyes. This may be the chance to take advantage of that short window of opportunity when little ones can be hugged and spoiled before becoming independent teenagers. When they live far away, as most of my eighteen do, it takes a lot of creativity, thought, and prayer to stay connected. Even the early teens, who don't seem to have much to say to adults, love to talk by email. I've sometimes entered their chat rooms! And nothing moves my heart more than to have one call and say, "Grandma, please pray for me."

The fourth quarter can be a time for "generativity"—time to pass on our wisdom and our experience to the next generation, to leave behind a legacy for those coming after us. Mentoring and grandparenting are two fulfilling ways to use these precious bonus years.

Leaving a Hard-Copy Legacy

How often have you said, "I wish I'd asked my grandmother about her childhood when she was still alive"? Just from listening to family conversations I know that my grandparents lived in Poland before the First World War, that my grandfather was sent to Siberia by the Russians, and that Grandmother and her five children fled to Berlin in a packed refugee train. But all the tantalizing details of her life, her suffering, and her faith have been lost forever. She never wrote anything down.

Every one of us has a story to tell, and if we are followers of Christ, we have the added dimension of reviewing his faithfulness over the years. One of the lovely things about growing old is that those long-term memories seem to come back more and more easily, even when what happened yesterday dims. What a blessing to our own spirits to begin to pull those memories out of our minds and put them down on paper.

Dr. Janet M. Peifer encourages residents in the retirement center where she works to begin to do life reviews and to share them with each other. She sees value even beyond the preservation of memories for future generations.

> When we engage in a review of our lives it assists in preserving personhood despite falling victim to the ravages of the aging process. It can help us come to resolution about unfinished business in circumstances and relationships. And it is an enriching source of wisdom for the family and congregation. . . . The unwritten history of many older persons and that of their congregations, families and communities is tied up in the memories of persons who will no longer be living in ten years or less.[11]

In the focus groups, one of the common responses to what they were doing in retirement was that women were writing their memoirs. One woman told of going through her mother's things and finding ancient pictures and old love letters from her grandfather. She made copies and put these together for each of her children for Christmas. Another told of encouraging her depressed mother, for whom she'd cared for fifteen years, to write her memoirs. As the daughter typed out each chapter she was fascinated with the stories of childhood and adolescence she'd never heard, and she decided it was time to start her own.

Identifying Our Passion

You'll notice that the interests that excite and energize us and give us a sense of meaning focus not so much on ourselves as on others. The Old Testament instructs us to love and serve God with all our heart (Deut. 11:13). We need to find our unique passion that causes our heart to race when we think of what God still has for us to do.

As I've asked women to identify their passions, I've realized there may be a misunderstanding about the meaning of the word. In the focus groups women responded with such subjects as exercise, travel, electronic games, maintaining their health, email communication, reading—even watching football. In a sense these do fit the definition of *passion*—a compelling desire that excites us and that we'd sit up talking about late at night.

At one time our family raised boxer dogs as a hobby. We took them to shows on occasion and met hundreds of other people passionate about boxers. They could talk endlessly about the length of the nose, the shape of the body, the coloring, and the perfect pedigree. One of our young boxers even won first in show, and we proudly brought home a certificate and a copper bowl. We made friends among the breeders and found that as long as we talked "dogs" we had a lot in common.

Our interest in dogs was a personal passion. It served as relaxation from the pressures of ministry and brought us into contact with people we would never have met otherwise. It gave our family a common interest and educated our five children in the "facts of life" as we bred dogs and raised puppies.

At the same time we were raising dogs, we were intensely passionate about the injustice we saw inflicted on the South African blacks. The unfair school system that failed hardworking students because of poorly trained teachers and watered-down curriculum disturbed us. We seethed at the injustice that kept a husband and wife apart because she didn't have a permit to work in the city. We could discuss these injustices with emotion and fervor well into the night, for we believed passionately that our African young people, created in the image of God, should be treated with dignity and equality. Non-Christians also were motivated by a fervent passion for justice, but without the tempering of the Holy Spirit this passion sometimes resulted in violence, deceit, and hatred.

While we loved raising dogs and the excitement of showing them, we had a far deeper and compelling passion—to see African young people freed from the injustices of the apartheid system and most important of all, free to serve God with the gifts he had given them. We found that we needed to control our time and interest in dogs lest that interfere with the overarching purpose God had given us.

Personal passions remain important even in our senior years. Whether it's raising dogs, gardening or reading, traveling or camping with our grandchildren, learning to dance or play bridge, passions add sparkle to our lives and connect us with other people. They can even form a bridge to the deep passion God has put in our hearts to bring glory to him.

An ultimate passion that comes from God is worthy of our life's best efforts. It is God-sized, bigger than personal desires or interests. It promotes God's kingdom and glory and can become the driving force of our lives. And it can change. My passion for justice for African young people has moved on through circumstances and God's call to a passion for women to be treated with justice and equality so that they can use their gifts to glorify him.

Bill Hybels in his book with Bruce Bugbee and Don Cousins, *Network: The Right People . . . In the Right Places . . . For the Right Reasons,* teaches that passion answers the question of where we should serve. "Passion is the God-given desire that compels us to make a difference in a particular ministry."[12] This does not refer to what is often called "full-time" ministry but to whatever area of service God has tuned our hearts.

Finding our passion may take some intentional introspection. Sometimes we find that our passions emerge as we accept a responsibility to serve or minister. When I first accepted the role of Women's Track Coordinator, I did not have a particular interest in working with women. Through prayer and discussion with Christians whose judgment I respected, I recognized that God was calling me to this responsibility. The passion emerged as I met women internationally, learned about the struggles and challenges they faced, and realized what an impact these women could make for the kingdom of God if they were released and trained for ministry.

Laurie Beth Jones in her book *The Path* suggests the following questions to ask yourself as you try to discover your passion:

1. What most excites you in or about your world?
2. What most angers you in or about your world?
3. If you could teach three things to others about what excites you in the world, what three things would you teach?
4. If you could convey to others three things about what angers you in the world, what would you convey?
5. How can you use what most excites you to affect or change what most angers you?[13]

I would add to these questions, "What concern has God placed in your heart that energizes you?" How you respond to that question will help determine whether you will finish well.

Nancy Miller discovered what enabled her to impact others after going through her deepest disappointment. It has become the revitalizing passion of her life.

Nancy Miller

Turning Wealth into a Godly Passion

> At some time or another we've dreamt about what we would do if we suddenly came into a large amount of money. Would our first response be to make sure our retirement was secure? Would we buy a bigger home? Or might we decide to give more to missions or respond to emergency needs?
>
> When we reach the age of retirement and realistically analyze our investments, no matter how much we have, many of us become apprehensive. We wonder, will my money outlast my life? Or will it be the other way around? At what point do we trust God and give generously? Or will we always be afraid to take risks?

Nancy Miller* doesn't feel she's taking a risk when she gives large amounts of her money to God's work. When she discovered the extent of her divorce settlement she was shocked.

"I knew immediately that it was the Lord's money. He's just asking me to distribute it," she says. Pausing, she adds thoughtfully, "The hardest thing is to know where to give it."[14]

A Humble Beginning

Nancy hasn't always been wealthy. In fact, born in the Depression years, she knew something of the financial struggle the economic downturn caused. She saw her parents move from

*Names and places changed throughout for protection of privacy.

job to job wherever her father could get work as a printer. She attended a two-room school in Maryland until she entered high school, when they moved once again, this time to Oregon.

After just a year of college Nancy felt she needed to get out on her own, so she moved to San Francisco and took a job as a secretary in an advertising agency. She and her roommate, Alice, became good friends, and she often spent time with her and Alice's boyfriend, Dave.

An enterprising young man, Dave had new ideas bursting in his head constantly. Nancy admired his drive and ambition, but she soon noticed that Alice and Dave were not getting along. After they broke up, Dave began to date Nancy. It didn't take her long to realize that she'd found in Dave the special man she'd been waiting for, and a few months later they were married.

"Dave became a very successful businessman," Nancy explains. "He learned some things about positive thinking from his Christian Science background that stuck with him over the years. He had gone to church every Sunday as a child, doing everything Christian Scientists do. But by the time he was eighteen he turned away from the church. He didn't believe what it taught anymore."

Nancy herself grew up in a hodgepodge of religious beliefs. Her father belonged to an Assemblies of God church. "It was very strict," she recalls. "No makeup, no movies. But Dad always loved God."

Her mother, on the other hand, grew up in a Catholic church in the days when Catholics and Protestants had very little to do with each other. It was not surprising that Nancy's mother didn't get along with her Protestant mother-in-law, who felt that her son had disgraced her by marrying a Catholic.

"My mother wouldn't go to an Assemblies of God church— and Dad wouldn't go to the Catholic church, so as a family we became Methodists. I was baptized in the Methodist church at thirteen. It was just something you did."

Nancy remembers going with her Dad one night to his church. When she heard the music and saw the worship she was shocked.

"I was all big-eyed. It reminded me of what I had heard people talk about 'Holy Rollers.'"

But in spite of her confused religious upbringing, Nancy always felt a love for God and a curiosity about the Bible. Several times she started reading in Genesis, but after a few chapters she'd become bored and put it away. By the time she met Dave she had gotten away from church altogether, and they began their married life without Christian fellowship or biblical teaching.

Back to the Bible

One day after they'd been married for about five years, a neighbor invited Nancy and Dave to their church. She and her husband had just become Christians and were eager to share their faith. Reluctantly Dave agreed to go. Just a few days later the pastor came to visit. Nancy remembers every moment of that meeting as the pastor explained the way of salvation to them both.

"He laid out the plan of salvation as I'd never heard it before," she remembers. "Without hesitation I got down on my knees right there in the living room and received the Lord.

"But my husband didn't; he felt there was a lot of hypocrisy in the church. After the pastor left he told me, 'I'm going to be honest with you. You can go to church and do whatever you like, but I won't go.'"

Nancy recalls talking with Dave's mother, trying to explain who Jesus is. Her mother-in-law reiterated her Christian Science teachings, just what Dave had heard over the years—that Jesus was a good example, a kind of model.

"She told me that sin is not real," Nancy says. "I couldn't figure out what she meant. It's everywhere you turn."

Nancy continued to grow as a Christian. Over the years she became involved in Christian Women's Club and Bible Study Fellowship. She even taught a Friendship Bible Coffee to new believers, though she would be the first to admit that she doesn't see herself as a teacher.

"Leading up front is not where I belong. That was not my gift." When asked what her spiritual gifts were, Nancy admits that she never felt she had a calling or really knew what God wanted her to do. "I've been an encourager to friends who've gone through tough times. But I've never discovered my spiritual gifts."

When the boys, Jay and Carl, came along a few years later, Nancy was perfectly happy staying at home caring for them. She took them to Sunday school at a nearby Presbyterian church. Jay became strong in his faith and was vitally involved in church activities, but Carl seemed less interested and gradually drifted away.

A Prosperous Business

Early in their marriage Dave kept seeking new business opportunities. One day a friend asked him to help build a new store he was opening. As they worked on the project together, Dave could envision the business growing through franchises, eventually across the country. Nancy knew little about his business affairs, but she sensed Dave's excitement and the possibilities for the future.

"I just encouraged him to go for it," she explains, "though I had absolutely no business acumen in any sense of the word. As his business increased, Dave gave me a very generous allowance, but he continued to handle all our finances and write all the checks."

The business grew rapidly into a very successful chain of stores across the country. Though Nancy had no idea of the real worth of their business, she knew there was plenty of money for their needs and more. Yet because of Dave's diffidence toward the church, she never felt comfortable asking him for money for the church or other projects she was interested in. She managed to give what she could out of her allowance. No doubt the leaders of her church must have wondered about her seeming lack of generosity, knowing Dave's successful business and their evident wealth.

Nancy explains it this way. "I knew that my husband was not interested, so I didn't really ever ask him to give large amounts of money. I had no control, and I felt shy about asking for a lot of money from him."

Over the years Nancy learned about Christian organizations she admired and respected, and many times she wished that she could give more—give enough to really make a difference.

End of a Marriage

At sixty-four years of age Nancy faced the deepest pain and depression of her life. Up to that point her life had seemed fulfilling and satisfying. She enjoyed her luxurious home and the opportunities to travel with her successful husband; she was proud of her children. Though Carl had dropped out of church, he had deep compassion for the needs of the poor and needy. Jay had married a Christian girl whom Nancy dearly loved, and she enjoyed spending time with her grandchildren. She had enriching friendships and challenging Bible studies that kept her growing in her faith.

But she sensed that something was wrong in her marriage. Though Dave had always worked long hours he had become more distant and preoccupied. Her suspicions grew, though she tried to suppress them. Finally after a year of anguished denial, she confronted him about another woman—and he left. After thirty-six years of marriage Nancy was alone.

"Divorce is worse than death," Nancy confessed. "If your husband dies it's over. But I felt as though half of my heart had been torn out. I had friends who were wonderful; friends who could identify. You go through stages of bitterness. Your self-esteem is very low, but only time can heal.

"There's a lot of loneliness, because married couples do things together. Out of courtesy they would invite me to things, but I'm not comfortable with married couples. The first four to five years were hard. I just didn't accept it. I kept thinking that he might come back. I finally realized after some time, that he won't." Even as she spoke these words her eyes reflected the pain and hurt she'd experienced and still returned to haunt her at times like a replaying nightmare.

With no-fault divorce rules, state laws divided Dave's assets down the middle. In her bewilderment and confusion Nancy turned to her sons for help. When they explained the extent of the resources she now had, Nancy could hardly believe it. She had had no idea how much money they had. It was almost beyond her comprehension. "When my sons made clear to me the depth of the amount, I began to realize, this is not for me to keep," she says.

She never questioned that the money was God's. She realizes that for some people the more they have, the more they think they need. She knows people who own three and four magnificent homes and for whom accumulation is their goal, regardless of their needs.

"If God hasn't satisfied your heart, then there's constant need. People keep wanting more and more," she asserts.

The Gift of Giving

With her sons' help Nancy formed a Christian foundation with clear goals and objectives, and almost immediately opportunities to give funds away arose. Nancy has learned how to use these resources wisely, to study projects carefully, and to distribute funds judiciously over a period of time. She wants to ensure that her money can keep giving for many years to come. Now the organizations she'd admired and wanted to help over the years have become targets of her generosity. She also believes it's important to encourage small new ministries, though she demands they prove their viability and impact.

"You can't always give what people ask," she says. "If Jay had his way, I think he'd give everything away. I feel I have to be responsible. I like to set up a certain amount at the beginning of the year, in different categories."

She believes that the Lord puts certain needs on each person's heart so that the money is distributed wisely for the furtherance of the work around the world. One of her concerns has been to learn more about how she can help with the AIDS crisis in Africa; she has attended conferences on AIDS and reads to keep herself informed.

Nancy is grateful for Jay's help. As the foundation grew he offered to leave his job and serve as its director. She recognizes that older women often need someone to help them unless they have handled their finances over the years. She wonders what she would have done without her trusted sons to guide her.

Nancy admits that she has retained enough personal resources so she doesn't have to worry about running out. To come to that conclusion she consulted an attorney she trusts, as well as discussing everything openly with her children. She knew that they had her interests at heart and would give her loving counsel. Furthermore, she wanted them to know what she was doing so there would be no surprises when God called her home.

"Older women with money, even limited amounts, have to be careful of scams," Nancy says. But she also senses that women become less secure about their financial future as they grow older, especially after they become widows, and that's why it's important to have wise consultants whom they can trust. As she has learned, it's possible to know how to figure out how much is enough to last their lifetime so they can give the rest away as good stewards of what God has given them.

Nancy is careful to ensure that what she gives is managed properly and used where it is designated. She demands full accounting and likes to see the projects for herself if possible. She has visited ministries in Africa several times and has come back with a whole new perspective of a continent she knew very little about before. At her age she was grateful she didn't have to sleep in grass huts or eat questionable food, but the contrast between her western way of life and the needs of the people was shocking. "I never knew what poverty was until I saw the women in Africa, many with AIDS, still trying to care for children who themselves were infected."

When asked what would encourage people to give more generously she replied, "Go! When you see the needs and the gratitude of people in other parts of the world, how could you not want to give? I think that seeing the things that are being accomplished with the resources you've given is the greatest joy. I always wondered why the Lord allowed me to have all this wealth. I realized from the start that it wasn't mine. He's put this in my hands. I think if more people could see what it does for others, they would be more generous with their money."

Nancy understands now that her spiritual gift is giving. God only revealed this gift to her in her senior years, but he'd prepared her heart to use it many years before.

EIGHT

TURNING YOUR HEART TO GOD'S PASSION

> Human life is not about human life. Nothing will go right in it until the greatness and goodness of its source and governor is adequately grasped. . . . Until that is so, the human compass will always be pointing in the wrong direction.
>
> Dallas Willard, *The Divine Conspiracy*

To this point we've considered the common concerns of all humanity as we grow older—dealing with our aging bodies, self-image, career opportunities, the changes and losses we face. But finishing well means much more for those of us who are Christ-followers, for our focus and interest goes beyond our own comforts and personal happiness.

Just as half of my world is out of focus without wearing bifocals, so my spiritual life is warped without also focusing on God's passion—that he be glorified through his children everywhere. Every believer in Jesus Christ potentially glorifies the Father.

Paul reminded his young protégé Timothy of this: "He wants not only us but *everyone* saved, you know, everyone to get to know the truth *we've* learned: that there's one God and only one, and one Priest-Mediator between God and us—Jesus" (1 Tim. 2:4–5 MESSAGE).

So whether we're preparing for the second half of life or are already enjoying the benefits of our bonus years, the desire that God's passion becomes ours enriches our lives as we honestly seek to glorify the Father above everything else.

Of course we can simply mouth these words in our routine prayers, but to glorify God through our lives requires that we intentionally show his love, compassion, mercy, righteousness, and truth—all that he is to us through Christ. When we demonstrate living our life as Christ would do if he inhabited our bodies (and isn't he?), we become true disciples.

God expects us, his children, to reveal his glory to the people around us, both our brothers and sisters in Christ and those who don't know him. David understood God's passion when he wrote: "Sing to the LORD, praise his name; proclaim his salvation day after day. Declare his glory among the nations, his marvelous deeds among all peoples" (Ps. 96:2–3). As king of the Jews, God's covenant people, David understood that one day God's glory would be revealed to all nations.

In *Let the Nations Be Glad,* John Piper challenges his readers to focus on worshipping God in all his majesty, confident that the zeal for reaching the nations will follow. He writes, "All of history is moving toward one great goal, the white-hot worship of God and his Son among all the peoples of the earth."[1]

We long to find meaning and purpose in our senior years. What better time to enlarge our passion for people near and far who are without Christ and to be available to help them see God's glory as he directs us?

Reaching the Neighborhood

It starts in our neighborhood where we pass people on the streets and in their driveways. Do they see enough of God's glory in us to wonder what's so great about Christianity?

When Mary Lance Sisk, chairperson of the Lighthouse Facilitation Council of Mission America, moved into her new neighborhood, she began prayer-walking. Before long several other believing neighbors joined her as they prayed for each house on the street. They used a neighborhood directory that contained a map of the neighborhood and a list of all the names, including the children. Soon they had seventeen women praying together, meeting monthly to share their experiences and to pray for their neighbors. Out of this small beginning a national Love Your Neighbor movement started. The women formed prayer-triplets[2] to pray for specific friends and neighbors; they held evangelistic teas and neighborhood Bible studies and saw many neighborhood families come to Christ.

In *Love Your Neighbor as Yourself,* Sisk wrote: "Opening your heart and home is not difficult once you realize that you are not responsible for converting any of your neighbors to faith in Christ. Conversion is God's business. You are called to love your neighbor and to offer your neighbor the opportunity to hear the gospel and to study the Word of God with you."[3]

Carole, one of Mary Sisk's prayer partners, tells of the exciting results of their prayer. In 1991 she was the only Christian in a new neighborhood of seven homes. By 1998 the number of homes had increased to thirty-two, sixteen of which had believing families. She's convinced that her prayer-triplet upheld the work that God was doing, and their prayer-walking cleared the way as they claimed the very ground for Christ.

Beyond our immediate neighbors we can focus on international students, immigrants, and refugees in our community. When an Afghan refugee mother moved into our city, a number of women from a local church visited the mother, who didn't know any English. In sign language and basic words they helped her write her first check, phone her family back in Kabul, and get her children started in school. Within six months she was speaking halting English; she agreed to attend an Easter service and accepted Christ.

Such opportunities to show compassion to people from other nations are endless, but we need the "white-hot worship of God" to convict us that showing his glory to them is worth more than our comfort or pleasure. The added benefit is that most Third World people admire and respect age, and the older we are the more likely they will be to listen to what we have to say.

Opportunities Overseas?

In my research and focus groups I found that many women look forward to some kind of involvement in overseas missions, beyond serving on the church missions committee or attending mission banquets. Many indicated that they plan to go on a short-term missions trip.

While mission fields profit from the offering of our gifts and ministry, the greatest benefactors of most short-term trips are generally the volunteers who go. Seeing the realities of life in other parts of the world—bonding with a single mother struggling to feed her family in Guatemala; experiencing the exuberance of worship in an African church; understanding the bondage of women in Muslim countries; learning about intercessory prayer from the Koreans—will change your attitude forever.

Many of us have skills, experience, and training that are appreciated in a short-term situation. Countries such as China and Afghanistan need English teachers. The benefits of years of experience in business can be transmitted to other cultures, especially where women are rapidly moving into the business world overseas. Christian leaders in the Arab world have asked for help for the women in their churches. Some are encouraging women to take a more proactive role in the church, but they need leadership training and guidance in developing study habits, public speaking, and writing skills, for few have had those opportunities.

Older volunteers haven't always been welcomed by mission organizations. The first trickle of senior missionaries emerged in the eighties. Previously mission agencies were cautious about sending anyone over forty years of age on international assignments. They worried about failing health and strength and inability to learn the language or adapt cross-culturally. But as numbers of younger candidates dwindled and health concerns diminished, agencies began to open their doors to seniors. And they found in many cases that senior missionaries had advantages over younger recruits.

One Middle Eastern missionary told me, "Send us older adults any day. They are so teachable and willing to do anything they are asked to do." The International Mission Board of the Southern Baptist Conference currently numbers among its missionary ranks more than three hundred "finishers" over fifty, serving three-year terms.[4]

Peggy Hanley always wanted to be a missionary. Her husband had originally planned to retire early and they dreamt of going overseas together. But a family business failure put those dreams on hold, and at fifty-two Peggy had to get a job. For ten years she worked as a physical therapist and continued to teach women's Bible studies on the side. In 1998, when she was sixty-three, God opened the door for her to go to the Ukraine with BEE (Bible Education by Extension) to train women in leadership in their churches. For five years she traveled three times each year, staying to teach a month at a time, and she trained more than five hundred women to train others.

In 2003 Peggy traveled to Vietnam to teach pastors' wives. Under the watchful eyes of the communist authorities, Peggy played the role of a tourist, meeting secretly with groups of women in their homes. She admits it was difficult and that she got extremely tired. It was emotionally draining to know that at any moment her classes could be discovered and her students arrested. She says she is ready to go again as long as her husband keeps working to support her habit.

If you sense God nudging you in this direction, look for information about opportunities for seniors. *Into All the World Magazine* annually publishes information about hundreds of mission and parachurch organizations with short- and medium-term mission opportunities, which you can access on their web site.[5]

Finishers Project,[6] for example, links people over fifty with both short-term and second-career missions opportunities. Finishers helps adults move from their current or past careers into missions service in conjunction with over seventy leading mission agency partners. Their requirements aren't as stringent for a two-week trip as for a year, but all have to be FAT—faithful, available, teachable. You can fill in a personal profile on their web site. Finishers also provides information about hosting a Finishers Forum at your local church.

Is Missions a Mandate?

We all know women like Peggy who have longed to make their bonus years meaningful and have taken risks so that God's glory would be revealed among people in another country. This doesn't mean that this is God's plan for each of us. Neither the glamour nor the need for a change from a mundane life justifies going overseas without clear and definite direction from the Holy Spirit. But the desire to see God glorified in the "one quarter of the world's population that has never heard of Jesus Christ" is incumbent upon us all.[7]

Jesus' last words on earth to his disciples reinforce the call: "You will receive power when the Holy Spirit comes on you; and you will be my witnesses in Jerusalem, and in all Judea and Samaria, and to the ends of the earth" (Acts 1:8).

Jesus was not giving us an either/or command, that our passion should be *either* for our city (Jerusalem), *or* our country (Judea), *or* ethnic peoples (like the scorned Samaritans), *or* the world (to the ends of the earth). Rather, he expects every Christian to have a local/global concern, no matter where his or her specific call might be, for God's passion is for the whole world.

One and a quarter billion people in the world have yet to hear how to glorify God through obedience to his Son. More than 90 percent of these "unreached people" live in what is known as the 10/40 window—the area between ten and forty degrees north, reaching from Western Africa across Asia, which is home to the three major non-Christian religions: Islam, Hinduism, and Buddhism.

What better way to utilize our bonus years, extra time, and financial resources than to be available to serve wherever he calls us? Those who have taken the post-retirement plunge are often ecstatic about their experiences.

Beth Rice wrote the following testimony: "When my pastor/missionary husband died in 1991, I was eighty years old, but I knew I could never really resign to being a stay-at-home missionary. So when I read in the *Fellow Workers* that an MK [missionary kid] teacher was needed in Cuenca, Ecuador, miracles big and small began to happen—renters for my condo, and my visa and birth certificate came through the very last day before we had to pick them up.

"I learned to teach and love nine MK's and the other devoted missionaries. . . . Then in 1992, I read of the need for a nurse/teacher in the . . . South African Pre-School Teacher's Training School for three months. . . . I began praying, 'Lord, do you want me to go?' That's a dangerous prayer to pray if you really mean it. . . . On a snowy second of January, 1993, I traveled to the Sea-Tac Airport. . . .

"Then when I was eighty-five and starting to think I was ready for retirement, I got a nudge in the form of a letter from Campus Crusade for Christ. There was an urgent need for a Teacher of ESL and Nursing in Budapest, Hungary; but would they risk an octogenarian?? Yup, I passed my physical and spent a most enjoyable eighty-sixth birthday at the International Christian School of Budapest. . . .

"Many ask: 'Now where?' And I reply: 'I'll go, if you'll go with me!'"[8]

How to Be a World Christian

One need not travel overseas to be a "world Christian"—a believer who shares God's passion that he be glorified in every nation, people, and language. Here are some ways we do it.

1. Reading the news or watching television gives us fuel to pray about what is happening and for people's needs. Our reading list includes the latest mission books and periodicals so that we can better pray for and understand missions in the twenty-first century.

2. Sometime along the way we'll take the Perspectives course, a fifteen-week in-depth study of mission history and strategy. Ministry experts have taught Perspectives to over fifty thousand people since 1974. You can contact the U.S. Center for World Mission for information about the course in your area.[9]

3. We give mission biographies to our grandchildren and tell them stories about children in other countries who don't know Jesus. And if we go on a short-term mission trip we enthusiastically tell them about it and might even take one of them with us! They know Grandma would be happy if God called them to be missionaries.

4. We evaluate the skills we've developed over the years and are willing to respond to a need for volunteers in local mission offices. If we feel God's nudge to utilize our gifts in some aspect of missions we're willing to persistently look for the "right fit" even though it may take time.

5. We become mission mobilizers in our church, Sunday school class, or small group Bible study. We bring news about God's kingdom-building program to our fellow believers for prayer or involvement. We offer to help on the church mission committee, take missionaries to lunch, and promote the cause of the missionaries our church supports. We might even invite a visiting missionary to our home for dinner or to stay with us.

6. As a world Christian we constantly look for ways to be involved in sharing Christ with those who don't know him, whether our unsaved neighbor, the immigrants in our city, or unreached people in another country.

7. We use our creativity like the women in Minneapolis who have made hundreds of lap-quilts so poor women in the Ukraine can attend unheated churches in the winter or

like the group in California who make dolls for girls in orphanages in Moldova. We respond to God's question to Moses, "What is that in your hand?"(Exod. 4:2) by offering what we have to God.

8. As world Christians we practice balanced stewardship, ensuring first of all that we are giving the proportion of our income God intends us to give, and that a part of that goes to the poor and the unreached. We will keep in mind that 96 percent of all religious giving in the U.S. remains here; 3 percent goes to nations that already have a small but viable church and only 1 percent to people in the 10/40 window, most of whom have never had an opportunity to hear the message of salvation.

9. Above all, we pray, for "the least we can do is the most we can do."

Prayer — Partnership with God

Paul writes, "We are God's fellow workers" (1 Cor. 3:9), and we are enjoined in Scripture over and over to pray.[10] My understanding is somehow enhanced as I obey God's instructions to pray, and my faith is strengthened as I see him glorified through my prayers.

Dallas Willard writes, "Prayer frequently requires much effort, continuous effort and on some matters possibly years and years of effort. Prayer is above all, a means of forming character."[11]

We watched one of our teenage granddaughters remain aloof to any spiritual influences in her life while in high school. She obeyed her parents to attend church, but she made it very clear she was bored and disinterested. Her father told me that he doubted she ever read the Christian books I sent her. Just before she left for college my husband and I invited her out for coffee, hoping there might be an opportunity to talk about the Lord. But the shades went down as soon as we began talking about the need for her to find Christian friends on her secular campus.

When she came home on a break from her studies, she told her parents about the drinking and sexual activities students engaged in, which disgusted her. Meanwhile her grandfather and I were praying every day that God would touch her life.

One weekend during her sophomore year she was invited to attend an InterVarsity Christian Fellowship meeting on the campus, and God broke through. She submitted herself to the Lord. What a difference in that young life! Since then she has led her roommate to the Lord and has gone on an outreach mission over Easter break. You can imagine how grateful we are to have had a prayer share in this holy revolution.

God-Sized Prayers

Often our most urgent prayers are about our daily needs: "Lord, help me to find a parking place" or "Don't let it rain on our picnic today." But as we desire his glory we will learn to pray with his passion.

When Jesus taught his disciples to pray, he included their daily needs such as food and protection from evil (Matt. 6:9–13). But most of his prayer dealt with the Father's glory, his kingdom, and his will.

James warns us, "You ask and do not receive, because you ask wrongly, to spend it on *your* passions" (James 4:3 RSV, emphasis mine).

"In prayer, real prayer," writes Richard Foster, "we begin to think God's thoughts after him: to desire the things he desires, to love the things he loves, to will the things he wills."[12]

Our prayers become more meaningful and powerful as we pray for others in the body of Christ, especially for the unity that Jesus himself prayed for so earnestly (John 17:23).

Paul gave us a beautiful model of how to pray for others in the body of Christ, whether for our children or grandchildren, our pastor, or our coworkers. "Praying Scripture" enables us to pray God's thoughts when we seem to be spiritually tongue-tied. Here's how I have prayed part of Paul's letter to the Colossians for a young man I met on a flight to Germany:[13]

> "For this reason, since the day we heard about you, we have not stopped praying for you and asking God to fill you with the knowledge of his will through all spiritual wisdom and understanding" (Col. 1:9).
>
> *Lord, since I met Robert I remember him each day, for he knows so little about you and has never read your Word before. Fill him with knowledge and understanding that comes from your Holy Spirit since he has no other Christians around him to help him.*
>
> "And we pray this in order that you may live a life worthy of the Lord and may please him in every way" (Col. 1:10a).
>
> *Father, in society today it will be difficult for Robert to live a life that will glorify and please you unless he finds other believers to help him grow. May he learn to please you and you alone.*

Focusing on an Ethnic Group

As we pray for the people of the world among whom God wants to be glorified, our reading and listening to him will help us zero in on special groups God wants us to pray for.

A number of years before the war in Afghanistan I began to be particularly concerned about the plight of women under the Taliban who were forced to cover themselves from head to toe in public and could neither attend school nor hold a job. My husband and I met a Christian who went back and forth into Afghanistan as a businessman. As a result we joined a small group of people who were praying specifically for the Pashtuns, one of the major ethnic groups in that land who are primarily Muslim. We met young couples eager to work among the Pashtun refugees in Pakistan, willing to take their precious little children with them. We prayed with a team taking hundreds of restored wheelchairs into the country where so many people had lost limbs because of land mines.

Then the war came; we prayed for victory over the Taliban and God answered. Nine Western Christian workers were arrested; we prayed for their release and God miraculously helped them to escape. We prayed that a "loya jirga," a meeting of the tribal leaders, would be held to form a government; the meeting took place and an interim government emerged.

We can't take credit that our prayers accomplished all these things. But we can rejoice that we partnered with God in what he wanted to do in that land, and we give him the glory.

Praying to the Very End

We can learn the discipline of intercessory prayer at any stage of life, but the earlier we start the better. It improves with age and practice. Even when our health fails and other abilities diminish, we can still partner with God in showing his glory to the world.

Evelyn Christenson has taught thousands to pray through her books and seminars. Reading her story will inspire you. Even though her health is failing she loves to praise her "Holy, Holy, Holy" Father as she's taught so many of us to do.

Let us pray:

> May the peoples praise you, O God;
> > may all the peoples praise you.
> May the nations be glad and sing for joy,
> > for you rule the peoples justly
> > and guide the nations of the earth.
> May the peoples praise you, O God;
> > may all the peoples praise you.
> Then the land will yield its harvest,
> > and God, our God, will bless us.
> God will bless us,
> > and all the ends of the earth will fear him.

> Psalm 67:3–7

Evelyn Christenson

CAN LIFE BEGIN AT FIFTY?

If you had told Evelyn Christenson at forty-nine that she would become a foremost Bible teacher, writer, and prayer leader around the world, she would have scoffed at the idea. Yet all this and more has happened since she stepped onto the stage of the second half of her life.

As a young pastor's wife and mother of three, Evelyn Christenson often felt she was on a fast-turning merry-go-round. Her husband, Chris, had accepted the call to a pastorate in Rockford, Illinois, in 1953 after his graduation from seminary. As the pastor's wife she balanced many plates at once—leading prayer meetings, answering constant phone calls, teaching Sunday school, and filling frequent speaking engagements.

In 1971 Bethel College invited Chris to serve on the staff. Evelyn had happy memories of Bethel, where she and Chris had been students, courted, and became engaged. But she didn't want to leave the excitement and rich ministry that had grown out of the women's prayer movement in the church in Rockford. She believed a wife should follow her husband's call, so she reluctantly agreed to the move to Minneapolis.

The reality exceeded her worst expectations. She felt as though she'd been put on the shelf.

"I thought God had lost his mind," Evelyn admits with chagrin. "For many months I was in depression. Chris traveled a lot for Bethel; the girls were in college and Kurt was in high school. I literally thought my life was done."[14]

She longed for the excitement and far-reaching impact of the prayer movement that had grown out of the fervent prayers of just three women.

Miracle in Rockford

Evelyn and her friends Signe and Lorna began praying together in 1964, ostensibly for the needs of the church. They started by confessing their own sins, and it was weeks before God gave them the liberty to pray for their church. It still moves her deeply to remember the revival that broke out in the church the next Sunday. She can see the young hippie, with beard and ragged clothes, falling on his face at the front of the church—and the hundreds of others who followed him, weeping, confessing their sins and accepting Jesus.

The ramifications of the women's prayers spread as the results became known throughout the denomination. Three years later the office of the Baptist General Conference called and asked Evelyn to conduct research for a six-month period on what happens when women pray. Evelyn hesitated, unsure about the assignment. One day in her devotions she read Revelation 3:8a, and the words jumped off the page as though God were speaking directly to her: "See, I have placed before you an open door."

She called the denomination headquarters and accepted the responsibility.

"I remember, after accepting the assignment . . . waking on that bitter cold and dark morning of January 1, 1968, knowing I had just six months to find the answer to that question. I did not have the faintest clue how to begin," she wrote. "As I lay in bed, horrified at what I said I would do, God showed me spiritually a door like a large trapdoor over my head. Assuring my racing heart that this was the answer, He said, *This is the door of prayer. It is praying—not studying about prayer, not analyzing prayer, not even sincerely believing My promises in the Bible about prayer—but actually praying!"*[15]

With this confirmation Evelyn began the prayer experiment. When they finally tallied the results, she wrote, "We had 66 pray-ers. From March to December, these 66 pray-ers prayed for 508 requests which multiplied to 33,528 prayers to God the Father [through the prayer chains], who sent back as many answers."[16]

As word of the prayer experiment spread, Evelyn was called to speak in many churches and denominations. The phone rang constantly, and the prayer chains grew.

Trusting in God's Promises

Now Evelyn's phone wasn't ringing; the invitations weren't coming; her stimulating class of professional people that she'd taught for fourteen years was no more. And she was about to turn fifty.

In the midst of her depression and self-pity, Evelyn clung to the promise God had given her in her early married life. Romans 8:28 had become her life's verse: "We know that in all things God works for the good of those who love him, who have been called according to his purpose."

How many times she had reminded God of this promise—when she had two miscarriages early in her marriage, when she delivered a stillborn baby, and again in the hospital when Judy was born with spina bifida and died seven months later. She and Chris praised God for their three healthy children—Jan, Nancy, and Kurt. The doctors had warned her that her last pregnancy with Kurt could cost her her life—but she had trusted God's promise and never once considered having an abortion.

"In all things God works for the good . . ."

Now in her depression and discouragement Evelyn continued to read her Bible faithfully. One day in her reading she couldn't move past 2 Timothy 1:6b: "Fan into flame the gift of God, which is in you."

Evelyn found herself asking, "What gift?"

She felt as though God yelled at her—*Prayer, of course.*

She remembered how in her thirties she had blurted out to God, "Lord, I want to teach the whole world to pray." Even today Evelyn feels a bit embarrassed about that presumptuous prayer.

"I didn't know what God was birthing in my heart. I begged God to forgive me. I said, 'Lord, I'm so sorry. Who do I think I am?'"

Now God challenged her again to teach others to pray, and soon after this encounter with God, she began a Bible study on prayer. The study grew into a weekend seminar.

Within two years after moving to Minneapolis, Evelyn had formed her United Prayer Ministries board and started a telephone prayer chain, both of which continue to this day. She began writing her book *What Happens When Women Pray,* which was published in 1975 and has sold over three million copies. It has been translated into more languages than she can keep track of. Evelyn has published twelve books, all written since she was fifty-three years old.

"I was so sure my life was done at forty-nine. I was in depression," Evelyn recalls. "But he had this plan; he had my board, my pray-ers. He had Viola Blake here who helped me write my first two books. What would I have done back in Rockford, not even close to an airport? God didn't make a mistake. When you get older you see that his timing isn't wrong. It's so awesome; faith in him is so important."

Faith had been planted in Evelyn's heart as a child. She saw her mother trust God and persevere with joy, even when her husband ran out on her. Evelyn accepted Jesus as her Savior at nine years of age in a Sunday evening service in Muskegon, Michigan. As a young child she prayed earnestly for the salvation of neighbors and friends who didn't know Jesus. She realizes that God had put a unique spirit of intercession within her even then.

God's Plan Revealed

Once Evelyn's book was published, the invitations began pouring in. Thousands of women attended all-day seminars to listen to this motherly looking little lady with the bright sparkling eyes and broad smile speak with compassion and power about how God answers prayer. At one time Evelyn had to turn down fifty invitations to teach for every one she accepted.

She depended on the power of focused prayer. Her telephone prayer chain chairperson called her three times a week for her prayer requests and by 6:30 the next morning the women were praying.

On her fifty-eighth birthday as she prayed for God's direction for the year ahead, Evelyn saw a vision of a hand holding a globe, stirring her heart once again to "teach the whole world to pray." Within two weeks she received an invitation to Australia and her overseas ministry began. For almost twenty years Evelyn mingled her North American seminars with her overseas teaching ministry, visiting every continent on the globe.

Wherever she went her books and tapes preceded her. "God distributed that book without our even trying. To us, getting *What Happens When Women Pray* in the hands of Christians around the world was the impossible task that we had not even tried to do. But to God it was as simple as someone sending a birthday or Christmas gift to a missionary; a military family's being transferred; someone whose life had been changed by prayer traveling overseas; or someone who had a similar vision from God and taught the book before moving to another country.

"In my deep gratitude, I have prayed so many times: 'I am so thankful God, that You do not limit Your answering to my ability to ask.'"[17]

In 1982 Evelyn received an invitation to come to India— thirty years after she and Chris had been appointed to serve as missionaries there. Their excitement at the prospect had turned to disappointment when the mission doctor refused to give them clearance because of Chris's bleeding ulcer.

Treatment in those days consisted of milk and cream—items the doctor was sure they would not be able to obtain in India.

"I cried every time our denomination would commission missionaries to India," Evelyn recalls.

On that first trip to India, thirty years later, Evelyn felt the power of focused prayer as one thousand pray-ers back home prayed round the clock for her. In a hotel room in Delhi she commissioned a young Indian woman, Juliet Thomas, who felt God calling her to train women in prayer and evangelism. Over the years this has become one of Evelyn's favorite ministries as she has seen Juliet form one of the largest women's movements in India, with prayer chains in more than one hundred cities. For many years Juliet produced a weekly radio program over Trans World Radio using Evelyn's materials.

On a later trip to India Evelyn gained access to a restricted state in North India. An Indian official back in the United States had inadvertently (at least so it appeared to the authorities) given Evelyn permission to enter Nagaland, which had been closed to foreigners for many years. But with the signed document in her hand, Evelyn was able to cross the border to find hundreds of women waiting eagerly for her teaching. When the officials discovered the mistake they told her she would have to leave immediately. "Immediately" turned out to be three days until the next plane left—long enough for her to finish teaching her three-day seminar. The twenty-four-hour prayer chain had done its work again!

Though Evelyn knows that "retirement" isn't in the Bible, the year she turned sixty-five she wondered whether she should "throw in the towel." Every year she prays for weeks before her birthday for a verse that will guide her to what God wants her to do next. That year her birthday verse was again Revelation 3:8: "I have placed before you an open door that no one can shut."

God seemed to be saying, *Where did you get the idea that it was your open door? If I open it, you can't shut it; if I shut it, you can't open it.*

She wrote out her birthday prayer for 1987 in the back page of her bulging, tattered Bible, which was liberally marked up wherever she'd received a word from God:

> Lord, I want to be that person who does only your will in all my relations, with my husband, my children, grandchildren, absolutely your will. . . . Father, I want to be like Jesus, only your will. Take me completely.

Two years later she found her birthday verse in Acts 9:15 where God reveals to Ananias what he was going to do with Paul: "This man is my chosen instrument to carry my name before the Gentiles."

Evelyn had been carrying the name of Jesus before the Gentiles (the non-Jews) around the world, but she wondered what more God had in mind for her. Nineteen months later she received her answer when she was invited to lead the AD2000 North American Women's Track.

The AD2000 Movement focused on the 10/40 window. Hundreds of churches, denominations, and mission agencies joined the movement to reach the goal, "A church for every people and the gospel for every person by the year 2000." The North American Women's Track (incorporated as Christian Women United) served as one branch of the global AD2000 Women's Track, which was just one of a dozen networks working toward that goal.

When the invitation came Evelyn's heart was already prepared for "something more." She accepted the responsibility to lead women in America and around the world to pray for those who had never heard about the love of Christ. For the next ten years, well into her eighth decade, she gave leadership, endless prayer, and her unique teaching gift to women.

She recalls, "When I turned seventy I didn't have enough strength. That year God gave Philippians 2:13 as my birthday verse: 'It is God who works in you to will and to act according to his good purpose.' God seemed to be saying,

Don't worry, it's God working in you. You don't have to have enough strength."

Evelyn understood. "He's not limited by my old body or my old age."

With that promise she wrote what is probably her crowning legacy, the *Study Guide for Evangelism Praying*, which incorporated all that she had learned and taught about prayer in one simple Scripture-filled manual. The AD2000 Women's Track facilitated the publishing of the original edition in more than forty-five languages, and hundreds of thousands of women around the world have learned about the cleansed life and triplet-praying for the lost.

How Evelyn Is Finishing Well

Sitting at the dining room table of a mutual friend, Evelyn and I spent several hours pondering what it means to finish well. In spite of her congestive heart condition, which causes her heart to work at only 30 percent capacity, she remains enthusiastic and excited about what God is doing in her life. At doctor's orders she's lost over forty pounds since I first met her ten years ago. Soft brown curls frame her round cheerful face, and few wrinkles give away that she's entered her ninth decade. She talks rapidly, moving from topic to topic without skipping a beat. She didn't even look at the pages of penciled shorthand notes she'd made for the interview. It seems she resonates with Corrie ten Boom, who in her old age and failing memory told Evelyn, "I don't forget a spiritual t'ing."

Evelyn has always been a woman of enormous energy and one of the most gregarious women I know. She told me that she just hates to sit on the shelf and thus keeps pushing herself, often beyond her physical strength.

In that regard she shared, "I gave God my body as a living sacrifice in 1965, and I've never taken it back. I know he'll use me no matter how weak I am, but I think he's just about used it up. There'll come a time when he'll say, 'thanks, honey.'"

An experience she had teaching Campus Crusade leaders illustrates her persistence in spite of physical weakness. An allergy had swelled both her eyes shut so she couldn't see her notes. But she taught for five hours with her face looking like a stewed tomato and totally from memory.

Evelyn's life reflects a combination of obedience to the Scripture and a positive attitude. "You either become bitter or better" is her philosophy.

She's concerned that she sees many older women willing to sit in their comfort zones. "Many want to be comfortable with their cup of tea, book clubs, fun things, travel. Their money goes for this, and they don't bother about somebody who doesn't know Jesus. I meet them all the time, those who say, 'I'm done.'"

When Evelyn gave a speech at the retirement service of a Christian leader she told him, "We're not giving you a gold watch. Jesus didn't say go and retire. . . . or go on extended vacations. When the steward did a good job, God gave the steward a bigger job."

You can't spend much time with Evelyn without knowing her passion to tell people about Jesus and to teach them to pray, which has never changed. She admits that for others their passions may change over the years. But she warned, "You better have some passion by the time you turn fifty."

She told the story of the man who was to have hand surgery. He asked the doctor, "Will I be able to play the piano after the surgery?"

The doctor replied, "Of course, you will."

Grateful, the man responded, "Oh good, I always wanted to play the piano."

Evelyn made the obvious application: "Having hand surgery doesn't make you a piano player. Don't expect some magic thing to fall when you turn fifty. The majority of people need to learn to pray earlier."

She made the point for Bible study and Scripture memorization as well. "Don't ask God to [help you] recall something you didn't study."

Evelyn and I talked about how she's feeling now that health and age have limited her travels and speaking.

"In 1979 my prayer was, God, you be glorified, not me. That was way back when *What Happens When Women Pray* was four years old. As I get older I am cautious that I never take his glory. God must get all the credit and glory. If I ever get to the place that I think that I've done it, or get some of the credit, I'm done.

"But," she added wistfully, "in the past I'd get acclaim. When you get old you don't have much of that. You can't do the big stuff. I filled the big halls; I don't do that anymore. The jobs are more humbling. When it gets humbling, you're just where you've prayed to be all these years."

Evelyn knows that God is shutting some of the doors. Because of her physical weakness she has to pick and choose, to prioritize which invitations she accepts. I realized it was a special privilege for me to have these two hours with her. She still writes, travels in the U.S., and teaches half-day seminars occasionally.

While she believes that her physical limitations are the most difficult part of growing old, she recognizes that many other compensations have emerged. She mused, "I'm probably unique in that as I have aged people have come to me for advice. Increasingly God has used me as a rudder in the body of Christ. As I've stuck to the Word of God and not denied Jesus, one by one Christian leaders have come to me to ask me about these things." She hesitated, wanting to be perfectly clear. "It sounds like pride. But when you know that you don't know, you know who does know. All of your wisdom, faith, and trust is centered on God."

Evelyn loves to talk and makes instant friends with anyone she meets. Part of her success as a communicator is her God-given gift of real love for people. But beyond the chatter and laughter, it becomes very evident that here is a woman whose faith has ripened into Christ-like maturity and who is determined to finish well.

NINE

How to Finish Well

To know how to grow old is the master-work of wisdom and one of the most difficult chapters in the great art of living.

Henry-Frederic Amiel, *The Journal in Time*

A pastor told me of an elderly woman in his church who spent years studying the Scriptures; he thought she probably knew as much about the Bible as he did. With her years of experience and knowledge she felt qualified to mentor younger women in the church and offered her services, but no one wanted her.

"They looked at the way she treated her husband, criticizing and degrading him in public," the pastor explained. "Her children had grown up to be rebels and wouldn't have anything to do with her. She may have had a lot of knowledge up here," he said pointing to his head, "but it never reached her heart."

Being a serious student of the Bible, though admirable, does not guarantee that we finish well. In fact, most of the qualifications of what we consider the "good life"—health, education, financial security, holding respected positions, being recognized for our talents—do not guarantee that we finish well.

Kathleen Fischer asks this poignant question, "Does anyone know how to live the last years meaningfully and joyfully?"[1]

Researcher George Barna found that one quarter of the adult population in the U.S. had no idea what would make their life successful. He found this attitude most prevalent among people fifty-five or older and individuals who had never attended college. Another quarter of the population considers some tangible accomplishments during life as a primary reflection of success. This most often entailed financial accumulation, educational achievement, or making a difference in the world.[2]

Scripture challenges the picture the media paints of a successful senior enjoying the rewards of smart investments with an endless round of entertainment and fun. In fact, Paul warns, "The widow who lives for pleasure is dead even while she lives" (1 Tim. 5:6). Even if we had the physical stamina and the financial means to spend our lives in travel, playing games, attending theatre and concerts, this could not answer Fischer's question—how *do* we live the last years of our lives meaningfully and joyfully?

Preparing to Finish Well

The answer to Fischer's question lies in how we prepare to finish well and whether we truly desire to live the way God intended. Of course, the earlier we start the better. Bob Buford writes in *Game Plan,* "The time to think about new avenues of useful activity is not when you're fifty-five or sixty, but when you're forty or fifty."[3]

This may generally be true, but throughout history many have accomplished their greatest works and have made their most profound contributions in their senior years. So don't let your age deter you from aspiring to utilize your gifts to the fullest. If God's Spirit is giving you a vision of a new thing, take the risk. Get involved and just do it!

More than this we must be intentional about waking up every morning asking, "How can I live today to fully glorify and obey the Lord?" We know that finishing well is a long-term process, so no matter what our age, the time to start is now.

God will honor our effort to at least finish well, and our desire to please and glorify him will keep us firmly on the path to the finish line. The writer of Hebrews warns: "It's crucial that we keep a firm grip on what we've heard so that we don't drift off" (Heb. 2:1 MESSAGE).

"Living on purpose is the only way to really live. Everything else is just existing,"[4] says well-known author Rick Warren.

Knowing that this purposeful living can continue until the Lord calls us home infuses our senior years with fruitful meaning. The prophet Joel includes women and the elderly—two groups of people who have often felt insignificant and unappreciated—when he declares, "Your sons and daughters will prophesy, your old men will dream dreams, your young men will see visions. Even on my servants, both men and women, I will pour out my Spirit in those days" (Joel 2:28b–29).

After many months of reading, studying, praying, and thinking, I've drawn up the following statement of how I believe God wants me to finish well. Perhaps after you've finished reading this book you will want to create your own statement. How to work out the implementation of this goal, of course, will be different for each person.

> To finish well I will intentionally and joyfully pursue the purpose for which God uniquely created me to the very end, trusting in every circumstance that he is always with me, faithful, loving, and strong.

I Will Intentionally . . .

How easy it is to slip into apathy or to resign ourselves to feeling that we have nothing to offer; that we are just in God's waiting room and have left our reading material at home.

I want to wake up every day asking, "God, what do you have for me today? How can I demonstrate the Christ-life within me here at home, to those I meet, or even on email today? What open doors of opportunity should I be ready to step into? How can I know you better and love you more?"

I've tried to resist the temptation to feel depressed or useless since I retired from a global ministry by intentionally and daily asking God to lead me. I recognize in myself that the desire to seek public ministry could easily overwhelm my longing simply to reflect God's glory, however he "shines on me."

I echo David's longing to walk in tandem with God: "Since my youth, O God, you have taught me, and to this day I declare your marvelous deeds. Even when I am old and gray, do not forsake me, O God, till I declare your power to the next generation, your might to all who are to come" (Ps. 71:17–18). David's powerful words have encouraged readers for thousands of years. He wrote them when he was nearing the end of his life, but he was still eager in his intention to tell those following him about God's power and strength.

Joyfully . . . in Every Circumstance

Ah! Here's the one I'm a bit shaky about. Can I really walk through the inevitable pain and parting that aging brings with joy rather than complaining, becoming depressed, or weakening my faith? I pray that I will be able to say with Paul, "Therefore I do not lose heart. Though outwardly I am wasting away, yet inwardly I am being renewed day by day. For my light and momentary troubles are achieving for me an eternal glory that far outweighs them all" (2 Cor. 4:16–17, changes mine).

We've seen this victory in the models we've read about: Vonette caring for her terminally ill husband; Joy enduring severe back pain; Ione living above the confines of being a caregiver. Facing daunting circumstances with faith and confidence not only provides meaning in the middle of difficult situations, it demonstrates that God is powerful and loving, just as he promised: "Even to your old age and gray hairs I am he, I am he who will sustain you. I have made you and I will carry you; I will sustain you and I will rescue you" (Isa. 46:4).

Pursue the Purpose for which God Created Me . . .

The temptation for those of us who are achievers is to feel that we must continue to achieve, to accomplish something, and to stay busy. Yet that does not assure we will finish well. For God may ask us to relinquish such human goals because he wants us simply to BE what he wants us to be. We may have to be just as intentional to find that elusive purpose God has designed in perhaps a quieter fashion. Here is where thoughtful reanalysis of our spiritual gifts comes into play. We need to remember that "each of us finds our meaning and function as a part of his body" (Rom. 12:5 MESSAGE)—for as long as we live.

Which of our gifts can be best used at this stage of life? We may have to curtail a gift of teaching because of lack of opportunity or physical strength. Does God have some new way for us to use that gift? Perhaps he wants us just to be available to a neighbor or share inspiration from personal study on the Internet or telephone.

A gift of hospitality usually requires energy, finances, and an accommodating home. Though these may be limited as we grow older, we can practice "extension" hospitality on a smaller scale. By offering a plate of cookies to a new neighbor, preparing a meal for a shut-in, or taking a lonely widow to lunch, we can continue to reach out in love to others.

Now that I'm retired from leadership, I find great satisfaction in listening to and encouraging my successor, Emily Voorhies. Our occasional "catch-up lunches" may serve as a mentoring session for her. They energize me to praise God for the years he allowed me to be involved in kingdom work globally and to pray for the continued progress in lives I may have touched.

On the other hand, God does not always allow us to downsize our ministry. He may ask us to keep on teaching as Evelyn Christenson does at eighty-one years of age, or organizing a global conference as Robyn Claydon did in her late sixties. While I've finally admitted that my value does not depend on doing some major ministry, I cannot refuse to take on such a responsibility if God calls me to do so—even though physically and emotionally I might wish to step down.

As we grow older we may find it more difficult to feel that we were created in the image of God. Sometimes it seems we've been reduced to unproductive drones, shriveled organisms that have lost their charms. I have seen older women, bent over and unobtrusive, living on the fringes of life, not aware that their Creator has given them worth and dignity. When God appeared in bodily form, he imparted a high value to the body—at any stage.

On the other hand, we've all seen women in their later years holding their heads high with a sparkle in their eyes, assured that they are daughters of the King and bear his DNA.

A pastor once held a twenty-dollar bill in front of his congregation and asked who would like to have it. Everyone raised his or her hand. Before giving it away he proceeded to crumple it into a ball and asked again, "Who wants this?" Again hands flew up. He then threw it on the floor and ground it into the carpet with his shoe so that it was not only crumpled but dirty. Yet everyone still wanted the bill. They knew that its value lay not in its crumpled appearance but in the power behind it.[5]

When we fully comprehend our value because we have been uniquely created in God's image and he loves us, we can embrace life with enthusiasm. Even when we grow old and weak, there can be a kind of shining about us, since we reflect the most glorious One.

God Is Always with Me

Basic to our ability to finish well is a biblical theology of God. Like Job, we need a "big view" of God, beyond the circumstances of our lives that we don't understand.

"If you do not stand firm in your faith, you will not stand at all" (Isa. 7:9b). With that warning we need to remind ourselves, with David, "I trust in you, O Lord: I say, 'You are my God.' My times are in your hands" (Ps. 31:14–15a).

Our faith and confidence lies in the One who is both loving and strong (Ps. 62:11–12a). When we face difficult tests, the temptation is either to say that God does not love us or he would not allow this to happen; or we may believe that he is not strong enough to handle such a big problem. To finish well we choose faith—faith that God has purposes we may not understand; faith that "in all things God works for the good of those who love him" (Rom. 8:28a).

And we focus on the hope we have in Christ. "We fix our eyes not on what is seen, but on what is unseen. For what is seen is temporary, but what is unseen is eternal" (2 Cor. 4:18). We rejoice in the hope of eternity because of the loving sacrifice Christ made on the cross. The older we get, the nearer we are to the fulfillment of our faith. When he was in his nineties, my brother-in-law, Glen, remarked joyfully, "We aren't rowing with our backs to the shore anymore."

Being a Godly Influence

Whether we know it or not, we influence the people around us, and we need to evaluate the impact we will leave behind. What do I as a woman of God want to model for those God puts in my path, especially my children and grandchildren? They will not remember my books or public speeches but how I showed them love and how practically I demonstrated my faith.

I dedicated this book to my twelve granddaughters, hoping in the years ahead they will look back and say, "Grandma finished well."

Dallas Willard defines character as "the inner directedness of self."[6] Character traits tend to solidify as we grow older, but with the help of the Holy Spirit and self-discipline we can work to change what is unlovely. We desire to leave a sweet aroma of Christ, which exudes thanksgiving, praise, joy, and peace.

The women in one of the focus groups interviewed live very frugally in a low-income area. When asked how they plan to finish well their answers all pointed to character:

I want to be a nice old person, full of faith, patience, unselfish.

I want to be remembered as an encourager.

I want to be available to help others.

I want to let things roll off my back.

I want to learn to handle frustrations of decreased abilities.

I want to be content and enjoy the gift of today.

I want to be open-minded in all situations.

Several commented that they don't want to be remembered for being cranky or complaining. Tournier reminds us that "these tendencies . . . become more accentuated with each succeeding stage in their lives. . . . The kindly person becomes more so as he advances in age. The critical person now never stops grumbling."[7] Negative characteristics intensify unless with God's enablement we intentionally work on change!

As we read the stories of women who model finishing well, we find character traits they have fine-tuned over the years. Note the persistent vision of Eliza Davis George to share Christ with the tribal people in the interior of Liberia in the face of tremendous odds. Or the compassion of Mavis Nkosi for unruly inner-city children who tested her weariness. Or the sweet spirit of hope Blanche demonstrated in her last days in the nursing home.

When you consider the influence you are making, do you find areas of your character that you need to ask the Holy Spirit to help you change? You can't do it alone, and he won't do it without you, but together you can work toward victory over your weaknesses. After all, we are a work in progress, and we have a powerful advocate for change in Christ.

"It's in Christ that we find out who we are and what we are living for. Long before we first heard of Christ and got our hopes up, he had his eye on us, had designs on us for glorious living, part of the overall purpose he is working out in everything and everyone" (Eph. 1:11 MESSAGE).

Faithful to the Very End

With all the encouraging opportunities our bonus years give us, we must face the fact that death will ultimately greet us. My goal is to be faithful and responsive to whatever God asks of me to the very end. And when the day comes that I have no control over my life, my actions, or even my thoughts, I want to rejoice with the prophet who wrote, "Surely God is my salvation; I will trust and not be afraid. The LORD, the [dear] LORD, is my strength and my song; he has become my salvation" (Isa. 12:2).

Our son Randy, who had been a missionary in a Muslim country, spent hours on the telephone talking with converts and church leaders overseas when he stayed in our home while undergoing chemotherapy. He translated leadership materials. His eyes sparkled with dreams about the growth of the church and the potential he saw in new believers. He shared his vision with our neighbors who'd come in for tea. He wrote lengthy prayers on his computer as he sat in our kitchen watching the sun reflect off the mountains, and he laughed with glee as he sat out on our deck in an unseasonable spring snow.

He did not plan to die at forty-two. He fully intended to join his family back in his adopted land, but he was ready for God's call home. He pursued the purpose for which God created him till the very end. He now knows what is on the next page.

Paul Tournier speaks of life as the pages of a book we turn as each one fills up with experience. "It is easier to turn over a page of life when we have filled it right up. The Bible talks of the patriarchs who died in peace because they had lived their 'full span of years' (Gen. 25:8). . . . My page of death is not yet turned; I cannot turn it until I experience it."

Randy filled each page with what God had given him to do, and though the passage was difficult, his Master walked with him to the other side of the valley. The veil remains heavy on our side, so we don't know what greeted him over there, but we can be assured he lost only the limitations of his natural body.

Dallas Willard reassures us, "He will metamorphose our humiliating body, transforming it into a glory body like his, utilizing the power he has to make all things do what he wants (Phil. 3:20–21). When we pass through 'death' into God's full world—or 'our earthy tent is torn down,' as Paul elsewhere says—we are not thereby deprived of a body, any more than Jesus himself was. Rather, we are then 'clothed with a dwelling place of the heavenly sort' and 'not left naked' (2 Cor. 5:1–8). The mortal part of us is 'swallowed up by life.'"[8]

We do not eagerly anticipate the act of turning that last page. We are naturally reluctant to face death and ignore talking about it. But we know we will all face this. Part of finishing well is to make those preparations for our departure that will enable us to face eternity with joy and make it easier for those left behind. Ultimately to finish well is to live life so in love with Jesus, so aware of the glory of God, so desirous of his will and seeing his face that when the time comes to turn the last page, we do not fear but recognize that the best is yet to come.

I couldn't resist closing with the story of Blanche Brittain, who experienced the reality of that life beyond at age 102 but left a sweet trail behind for us to follow.

Blanche Brittain

"JESUS LED ME ALL THE WAY"
(Based on personal memoirs by Ethel Herr)

Someday life's journey will be o'er, and I shall reach that distant shore I'll sing while entering heaven's door, Jesus led me all the way.

John Peterson

"How can you do this to me?" Blanche Brittain said accusingly to her daughter. Blanche looked so frail lying in the bed, her leg in a cast up to her hip. Alice wished she could undo her decision to place her mother in the nursing home. But at seventy-nine Alice could no longer care for her one-hundred-year-old mother, especially now that her mother had fallen and crushed her ankle beyond medical repair.

Assuring her weeping mother that they would be back in the morning, Alice and her daughter Ethel left with heavy hearts. Though the home had been highly recommended, they had found it depressing, peopled with pathetic specimens of once vitally alive humanity. To make matters worse most of the staff were foreigners who could speak little English.

Alice and Ethel could hardly hold back the tears themselves as they thought of their gentle, loving mother and grandmother so angry and distressed at what seemed like their deception. They admitted that up until now Blanche had been very little trouble at home, sleeping a good bit of the time.

Ethel recalls, "Most days I'd see her sitting in her rocking chair with her well-worn Bible in her lap, eyes closed, lips moving and emitting gentle swishing whisper sounds. 'She's praying,' Mother would always say."

But Blanche's fall had been the final straw that made Alice realize she could no longer care for her mother, lift her onto the commode, or respond to her nightmares. This decision was the "Christian thing to do."

Blanche had brought her children up to do the "Christian thing." She didn't know much about her own family roots, though she believed that her ancestors had crossed the country by covered wagon. They'd settled in Washington State in the nineteenth century.

When Blanche was only ten years old, her talented, artistic mother died giving birth to her fifth child. The children were scattered among relatives. Only Blanche remained with her father. She used to say whimsically, "Not Blanchie. I was too mean. Nobody would have me so I stayed home with my father."

Though the family had little evident religious background, God protected Blanche even in those early years. When a "sewing machine salesman" came to call one day while her father was at work, Blanche naively invited him in. But God protected her from a devastating experience.

Her father realized that he couldn't care for his little girl by himself, and he soon placed her in a Methodist minister's home where she served as a companion for his crippled son. In this God-fearing family Blanche first learned about the Bible and what it meant to trust Jesus. She went forward at a Billy Sunday tent meeting in her town when she was twelve years old.

Ethel knew little about her grandmother's early years. She knew she had married in her teens to Burt Brittain, who had felt sorry for her when another suitor jilted her. In spite of a questionable start, it was a long and happy marriage until Burt died in 1958. Blanche was seventy-two.

Blanche never had a "career" as we think of it today. She happily fulfilled her role as a loving wife and mother, a faithful churchgoer, an intercessor, one who loved the Word of God. And she knew she could sing—how she could sing. All through the years as she raised her three children Blanche sang in the Baptist church choirs. She had dreamed of being a professional singer, but with only a fifth grade education and little money for training, that dream eluded her.

Ethel describes Blanche as a model grandmother. "Grandma had always been there for me with her bright smile and cheerful laughter, her clever wit, and her open heart to listen. . . . She was warm and domestic. Besides her bell-like voice, she had an aromatic kitchen, an incredible imagination, a giant conch shell that let me experience the ocean in her living room, and a marvelous fat button jar with a mother-of-pearl lid. Most of all, she'd always channeled God's unconditional love in my direction."

After Burt died Blanche moved in with her daughter, Alice, for the mother and daughter were fast friends. Many an evening Alice would play the piano while Blanche sang the old hymns they both loved. When the two elderly women could no longer manage on their own, Ethel and her husband, Walt, invited them to live with her. Blanche's cheerful, uncomplaining spirit and sparkling smile made her an easy person to have around. She loved to watch football and basketball games on TV and cheered her favorite teams like a Monday-night addict.

As the years passed, Blanche became less active and more frail. But at her hundredth birthday party her clear soprano voice sang out the testimony of her life, "Jesus Led Me All the Way."

Just a few months later she fell and broke her ankle, and the difficult decision to place her in a nursing home had to be made. Blanche was angry and resentful; for a time she refused to speak to her daughter. Whenever Alice and Ethel visited, she'd ask Ethel, "When are you going to let me come home?"

But gradually a change came over her, and her usual cheerful self began to emerge. As she wheeled herself around the home she would sing the old songs to the people around her. At a Mother's Day party that year she sang a solo—"What a Friend We Have in Jesus."

One Sunday Blanche wheeled herself into the room across the hall to visit a newcomer—a man only in his forties with advanced multiple sclerosis. His wife sat beside his bed grieving, asking God whether she had done the right thing. Suddenly, piercing through her pain, came the beautiful voice and clear words as Blanche began to sing "How Great Thou Art."

Blanche not only accepted her situation but realized that God had given her a new place to serve him. She had actually discovered a purpose in her sojourn.

One day she announced to Ethel, "Of course I miss my home and I'd love to be with my family. But God has put me here for a reason. He has work for me to do. There are so many people that don't know him."

People in the nursing home loved Blanche, and the staff felt sorry for her because she had been placed in a room with a roommate who had dementia. Sometimes Lida would weep and scream, but somehow Blanche was able to quiet her down, often by reading the Bible to her or praying with her as she held her hand.

One day a nurse came to Blanche with some good news. A vacancy had occurred in another part of the building, and they were going to move Blanche to a nicer room with a more compatible roommate. But Blanche adamantly refused, "Oh no," she said, "I can't move. Lida needs me."

On her 102nd birthday a local newspaper, the *Santa Clara Sun,* printed a picture of a smiling Blanche enjoying her birthday celebration. The article quoted her as saying, "I'm just enjoying being 102. I have such good health. I thank the Lord I have such a wonderful life."

Some months later a male nurse called Ethel at home. "Your grandmother is acting strangely. She told us she is 'going home,' and I have a feeling she may fall asleep tonight and never awake." When the nurse had tucked her into bed and prayed with her, she interrupted his prayer to tell him, "It may take me a couple of days, but I'm going home."

When Ethel visited Blanche she found her lying quietly and semiconscious. Blanche acknowledged Ethel's presence but made only two statements. One was a fragment of Scripture: "The peace of God that passeth all understanding." The other was a line from a song she had sung regularly on her wheel-chair rounds: "The love of God is greater far, than tongue or pen can ever tell." Ethel joined in; Blanche's voice that had remained clear and beautiful for so long was now weak and hardly melodic.

For the next two weeks Blanche hovered between life and death.

Friends and family, staff and residents crowded into her room, wanting to spend these last minutes with the woman who had found purpose and meaning to her life right up to the very end. The last words anyone heard from her lips were, "The love of God is greater far."

Blanche had finished well and was welcomed into the arms of One who surely said, "Well done, my good and faithful servant."

Blanche's daughter, eighty-one-year-old Alice Funkhauser, wrote the following poem after learning she had Alzheimer's.

> Be with me when the road lies clear,
>   Or when the shadows tempt to fear;
> When in the light the trail I trace,
>   Or when I cannot see your face;
> When fearful, in a foreign land,
>   Or when I feel you squeeze my hand;
>   There is no map, no unknown place
>   For every walk is through your grace!
>
> *Dear Lord:*
> *Take this shaky old frame*
> *And do something with it*
> *To honor Your Name.*
>
> A.F.[9]

Appendix A

How to contact organizations on the Web that offer volunteer opportunities:

www.volunteermatch.org—Web's largest database for local volunteer opportunities.

www.seniorcorps.org—a publicly and federally funded organization; lists both nonprofits and faith-based organizations. The Corps includes the Retired and Senior Volunteer Program, Foster Grandparent Program, and Senior Companion Program.

www.Christianprimetimers.org or email Servant Opportunities at cap@servantopportunities.net. Servant Opportunities provides personalized profiles comparing your skills with a database of over eight thousand organizations.

APPENDIX B

Responses to the following question in the Fifty and Beyond Questionnaire: "What specific ministry/service do you think God expects of you in the years after retirement?"

Caregiver
Children at risk
Children's ministry
Chinese ministry
Church planting
Church work
Counseling
Encouraging moms
Encouraging pastoral families
Evangelism
Giving
Grandparenting
Health care advocate
Hospitality
Intergenerational ministry
International
Leading women's group
Make family priority

Make videotape
Mentoring
Minister to lonely
Missions
Nursing home
Pakistani families
Parachurch ministry
Pastoring
Phoning, writing shut-ins
Prayer
Speaking
Teach Bible study
Teach English to Japanese
Teaching in college
Teach Spanish
Travel
Volunteering at hospice
Women's shelter
Work with poor, homeless
Writing
Youth work

Appendix C

Principles for effective intercession—adapted from Joy Dawson's *Intercession, Thrilling and Fulfilling.*[1]

1. Praise God for who he is. God's power is especially released through worshipful song (2 Chron. 20:21; Heb. 7:25b).
2. Make sure your heart is clean before God by giving the Holy Spirit time to convict should you have any unconfessed sin Ps. 66:18; Ps. 139:23–24; Mark 11:24–25; Luke 17:3–5; Job 42:10; Gal. 5:6).
3. Acknowledge that you can't really pray effectively without the Holy Spirit's enabling (Ps. 24:3–5; Rom. 8:26b; Eph. 5:18b; Prov. 8:13).
4. Deal aggressively with the enemy. Come against him in the all-powerful name of the Lord Jesus Christ and with the sword of the Spirit—the Word of God (James 4:7).
5. Die to your own imaginations, desires, and burdens for what you feel you should pray (Prov. 3:5b; Prov. 28:26a RSV; Isa. 55:8a).
6. Praise God now in faith for the remarkable prayer time you're going to have.
7. Wait before God in silent expectancy, listening for his direction (Ps. 81:11–13; Ps. 62:5; Micah 7:7 RSV).
8. In obedience and faith, take action on what God brings to your mind, believing (John 10:27; Ps. 32:8).

9. If possible, have your Bible with you should God want to give you direction or confirmation through his Word (Ps. 119:105).

10. When God ceases to bring things to your mind for which to pray, finish by praising and thanking him for what he has done, reminding yourself that "... from him and through him and to him are all things. To him be the glory forever! Amen" (Rom. 11:36).

Notes

Introduction

1. Kathleen Fischer, *Autumn Gospel: Women in the Second Half of Life* (New York: Paulist Press, 1995), 149.

2. Jenni Parker, "Memorial Set as Christian Leaders Remember Bill Bright," *Agapepress: Christian News Service,* 22 July, 2003, http://headlines.agapepress.org/archive/7/222003b.asp (accessed 22 July 2003).

Chapter 1: Biblical Models: Facing the Future with Vision and Grace

1. George Barna, "Women are the Backbone of the Christian Congregations in America," *Barna Research Online,* 6 March 2000, http://www.barna.org/cqi-bin/Page Press Release.asp?Press Release ID=47&Reference=E&Key (accessed 28 May 2002).

2. Author's interview, 17 February 2003. All quotations unless otherwise noted are from this interview or Joy's personal comments later.

3. Joy Dawson, *Forever Ruined for the Ordinary* (Nashville: Thomas Nelson, 2001), 22.

4. Joy Dawson, *Intercession, Thrilling and Fulfilling* (Seattle: YWAM Publishing, 1997), 84.

5. Ibid., 188.

Chapter 2: Aging through the Ages

1. *Fifty and Beyond Questionnaire* (Colorado Springs: Global Action, 2002). Of 2,200 questionnaires sent to the *Women of Global Action* mailing list, 250 completed questionnaires were returned.

2. Brian P. Levack, *The Witch-Hunt in Early Modern Europe* (New York: Longman Publishing Group, 1995), 129.

3. Thomas Cole, *The Journey of Life: A Cultural History of Aging in America* (Cambridge: Cambridge University Press, 1992), 230–31.

4. Ruth A. Tucker and Walter Liefeld, *Daughters of the Church* (Grand Rapids: Academie Books, 1987), 274.

5. Ibid., 273.

6. Joint UNAIDS/WHO Press Release, "Impact of Aids Worsens African Famine," 26 November 2002, http://www.unaids.org/worldaidsday/2002/press/WAD02EpiPR_en.doc. (accessed 8 May 2003).

7. Elaine Partnow, *Breaking the Age Barrier* (New York: Pinnacle Books, 1981), 23.

8. Robert N. Butler, *Why Survive? Being Old in America* (New York: Harper & Row, 1975), 12.

9. Dale McFeatters, "Getting older and getting even," *Rocky Mountain News,* 29 March 2002.

10. Ibid.

11. Rosalynn Carter, *First Lady from Plains* (Boston: Houghton Mifflin, 1984), 283.

12. James Hillman, *The Force of Character and the Lasting Life* (New York: Random House, 1999), 15.

13. Ignatz L. Nascher, ed. *Geriatrics: The Diseases of Old Age and their Treatment* (Philadelphia: P. Blakiston's Son & Co., 1909), v-vi, quoted in Cole, *The Journey,* 202.

14. Carol Taylor, "Living Well Until We Die: Moral Imperatives for the 21st Century," paper delivered at the Conference on Aging, Death and the Quest for Immortality, Trinity International University, Deerfield, Illinois, July 2001.

15. Lorry Lutz, *When God Says Go: The Amazing Journey of a Slave's Daughter* (Grand Rapids: Discovery House Publishers, 2002). Originally published: *Born to Lose, Bound to Win* (Irvine,

Calif.: Harvest House Publishers, 1980). The complete story of Mother Eliza George.

Chaper 3: Growing Old in the Twenty-first Century

1. Ashley Montague, *Growing Young* (New York: McGraw-Hill, 1981), 5.

2. Bob Buford, *Game Plan: Winning Strategies for the Second Half of Your Life* (Grand Rapids: Zondervan, 1997), 20.

3. Administration on Aging, "Future Growth," *A Profile of Older Americans: 2002,* 19 March 2003, http://www.aoa.gov/prof/statistics /profile/2.asp (accessed 12 May 2003).

4. William Sadler, *The Third Age: Principles for Growth and Renewal after Forty* (Cambridge, Mass.: Perseus Publishing, 2000), 204.

5. Administration on Aging, "Health, Health Care and Disability."

6. Administration on Aging, "Living Arrangements."

7. Lydia Bronte, *The Longevity Factor: The New Reality of Long Careers and How It Can Lead to Richer Lives* (New York: Harper-Collins, 1993), 37.

8. Richard Restak, "All in Your Head," *Modern Maturity,* January/ February 2002, 60.

9. Lorry Lutz, *Women as Risk-Takers for God: Finding Your Role in the Neighborhood, Church and World* (Grand Rapids: Baker, 1998).

10. Janet Kinosian, "The Creators—How they keep going and going and . . ." *Modern Maturity,* March/April 2000, 44.

11. Fischer, *Autumn Gospel,* 2.

Chapter 4: How Baby Boomers Can Prepare for the Second Half of Life

1. Gail Sheehy, *New Passages: Mapping Your Life Across Time* (New York: Ballantine Books, 1995), 4.

2. Leslie Kennedy, "50 (plus) & fabulous," *Rocky Mountain News,* 10 August 2002, sec. E., pp. 4–5.

3. Author's interview, September 2002.

4. Buford, *Game Plan,* 57.

5. Partnow, *Breaking the Age Barrier,* 178.

6. Lutz, *Women as Risk-Takers for God,* 202.

7. Buford, *Game Plan,* 45.

8. Author's interview, April 2002.

9. C. Peter Wagner, *Your Spiritual Gifts Can Help Your Church Grow: How to Find Your Gifts and Use Them to Bless Others* (Ventura, Calif.: Regal Books, 1994), 34.

10. Laurie Beth Jones, *The Path: Creating Your Mission Statement for Work and for Life* (New York: Hyperion, 1996), xvii.

11. Author's interview, February 2002.

12. Author's interview, January 2003.

13. Lausanne Committee: The Lausanne Committee for World Evangelization (LCWE) is an international movement for the purpose of encouraging Christians and churches everywhere to pray, study, plan, and work together for the evangelization of the world.

14. Robyn Claydon, *Keep Walking* (Australia: SPCK, 2001), 127.

Chapter 5: Preparing for Difficult Transitions

1. Buford, *Game Plan,* 51.

2. Ethel Herr, *Lord Show Me Your Glory: 52 Weekly Meditations on the Majesty of God* (Camp Hill, Penn.: Christian Publications, 2003).

3. ALS—Lou Gehrig's Disease: a fatal illness that shuts down the muscles of the body one by one, usually resulting in death by asphyxiation as the lungs cease to function.

4. William Bridges, *Transitions: Making Sense of Life's Changes* (Reading, Mass.: Addison-Wesley Publishing Company, 1980), 9.

5. Ibid., 104.

6. Stephen Post, "Extended Lives in Hope and Despair," paper delivered at the Conference on Aging, Death and the Quest for Immortality, Trinity International University, Deerfield, Illinois, 19–21 July 2001, 2.

7. Russell Wild, "Someone To Watch Over Me," *AARP* January/February 2003. Article suggests that long-term insurance in the Northeast, for example, where costs are relatively high, is not necessary with resources below $150,000, since Medicaid would

have to cover costs anyway. Those with resources over $2 million could cover the cost of care. In-between it would be wise to have long-term insurance.

8. National Academy of Elder Law Attorneys, *Reforming the Delivery, Accessibility & Financing of Long-term Care in the United States*, January 2000, quoted in National Endowment for Financial Education, Long-Term Care Think Tank (Scottsdale, Arizona: 6–8 May 2001), http://www.nefe.org (accessed 14 May 2003).

9. Sally S. Stich, "Who Gets the Stuff?" *Time,* 20 January 2003, A2.

10. Ibid., A3.

11. Howard G. Hendricks, "Rethinking Retirement," *Biblotheca Sacra 157,* April/June 2000, 13.

12. Paul Tournier, *Learn to Grow Old* (New York: Harper & Row, 1972), 16.

13. National Endowment for Financial Education, Long-term Care Think Tank, *Our Next Financial Crisis* (Scottsdale, Arizona: 6–8 May 2001), http://www.nefe.org (accessed 14 May 2003).

14. U.S. Bureau of the Census, 1992, quoted in Jean Coyle, ed., *Handbook on Women and Aging* (Westport, Conn.: Greenwood Press, 1997), 419.

15. Ruth H. Jacobs, *Be an Outrageous Older Woman* (New York: HarperCollins, 1997), 171.

16. U.S. Census Bureau, quoted in *USA Today,* 1 July 1999, 1–2D.

17. April Holthaus, "Looking Back," *Survivors Hope,* April 2003, 6.

18. Tournier, *Learning,* 191.

19. Ibid., 92.

20. Ibid., 96.

21. Author's interview, November 2002.

22. Author's interview, March 2003.

Chapter 6: How the Church Helps Women Finish Well

1. Greg Waybright, "Local Church Ministry To and Through Older Adults," paper delivered at the Conference on Aging, Death

and the Quest for Immortality, Trinity International Seminary, Deerfield, Illinois, July 2001.

2. George Barna, "Generational Differences," *Barna Research Online,* 19 April 2001, http://www.barna.org (accessed 28 May 2002).

3. Win and Charles Arn, *Catch the Age Wave: A Handbook for Effective Ministry with Senior Adults* (Kansas City, Missouri: Beacon Hill Press, 1999), 52.

4. Ibid., 48–49.

5. Janet Peifer, "Dispelling the Myths About Aging and Ministry with Older Adults," (Unpublished paper, East Berlin, Penn.: September 1996).

6. Christian Association of Senior Adult Ministries, 227601 Forbes Rd. #49, Laguna Niguel, CA 92677; email: info@gocasa.org.

7. Author's interview, January 2003.

8. Coyle, *Handbook,* 235.

9. Author's interview, February 2002.

10. Barna, "Generational Differences."

11. Ibid.

12. Waybright, "Local Church Ministry To and Through Older Adults."

13. George Barna, "Women Are the Backbone of the Christian Congregations in America," *Barna Research Online,* March 6, 2000, http://www.barna.org (accessed 28 May 2002).

14. Win Couchman, *Don't Call Me Spry* (Wheaton: Harold Shaw Publishers, 1990), 7.

15. Ibid.

16. Ibid.

17. Ibid., 84.

18. Ibid., 55.

19. Ibid., 47.

20. Ibid., ix, x.

Chapter 7: Finding the Key to Fruitful Bonus Years

1. Ted Engstrom with Joy Page, *Add Life to Your Years: Aging with Passion and Purpose* (Wheaton: Tyndale House, 2002), adapted from 43–46.

2. Ibid., xiii.

3. Thomas Cole, *The Journey of Life, A Cultural History of Aging in America* (Cambridge: Cambridge University Press, 1992), 227.

4. Current Population Reports, "Poverty in the United States: 2000," pp. 60–214, September 2001, http://aoa.gov/STATS/profile/2001/8.html (accessed 11 August 2002).

5. *60 Minutes,* CBS, 12 January 2003.

6. Jimmy and Rosalynn Carter, *Everything to Gain: Making the Most out of the Rest of Your Life* (New York: Random House, 1987), 157–58.

7. William Sadler, *The Third Age: 6 Principles for Growth and Renewal after Forty* (Cambridge, Mass.: Perseus Publishing, 2000), 197.

8. Assemblies of God News Service, "Pilot Shows Plane, Shares the Lord," 30 November 2001, http://www.ag.org/top/news/news_article_template.cfm?ArticleID=5805&NamedFormatID= (accessed 5 December 2001).

9. Carter, *Everything to Gain,* 158.

10. For more information contact Cavin Harper at Lifequest, 5844 Pioneer Mesa Drive, Colorado Springs, CO 80918; (719) 522-1404; email: lifequest@GBRonline.com.

11. Janet M. Peifer, "Reflection Upon Lived Experience," September 1996, http://www.equalworth.net/ministry/aging/Psalm 71.htm (accessed 25 February 2003).

12. Bruce Bugbee, Don Cousins, and Bill Hybels, *Network: The Right People . . . In the Right Places . . . For the Right Reasons,* Participant's Guide (Grand Rapids: Zondervan, 1994), 14.

13. Jones, *The Path,* 50.

14. All quotations based on interview in February 2002.

Chapter 8: Turning Your Heart to God's Passion

1. John Piper, *Let the Nations Be Glad: The Supremacy of God in Missions* (Grand Rapids: Baker, 1993), 15.

2. A prayer-triplet: three people who commit to meet for at least fifteen minutes each week. Each one prays for the salvation of three other people in their neighborhood, workplace, or family, and for an unreached people group.

3. Mary Lance V. Sisk, *Love Your Neighbor as Yourself: Blessing Your Neighborhood Through Love & Prayer* (Charlotte, N.C.: Mary Lance Sisk, 1998), 44. The book is available from the author at P.O. Box 472247, Charlotte, NC 28247-2247, email: Msisk91242@aol.com.

4. Nelson Malwitz with Mike Pollard, "From the Marketplace to Ministry," *Mobilizer,* Fall 2002, 10–12.

5. Bill Berry, ed., *Into All the World Magazine;* email: intoall@aol.com; <http://www.aboutmissions.com>

6. Finishers, P.O. Box 926, Brookfield, CT 06804; (203) 740-7278; email: office@finishers.org; <http://www.finishers.org>

7. Todd Johnson, "World Christian Briefing," *World Christian News,* Issue 24, 2003, 14.

8. Beth Rice, "O the Sheer Joy Of It! Finishing Strong," *Fellow Workers* (World Mission Prayer League: July/August 2000), 21–22.

9. U.S. Center for World Mission, 1605 Elizabeth St., Pasadena, CA 91104; (626) 398-2125, http://www.perspective.org

10. A few of the many injunctions to pray in Scripture: Colossians 4:12; Romans 15:30; Ephesians 6:18; Romans 10:1; 2 Thessalonians 3:1; 2 Corinthians 1:11.

11. Dallas Willard, *The Divine Conspiracy: Rediscovering Our Hidden Life in God* (New York: HarperSanFrancisco, 1998), 250.

12. Richard Foster, *Celebration of Discipline: The Path to Spiritual Growth* (San Francisco: Harper Collins, 1978), 33.

13. Entire intercessory prayer—Colossians 1:3–14.

14. Unless otherwise noted, all quotations come from author's interview, November 2002.

15. Evelyn Christenson, *What God Does When Women Pray* (Nashville: Word Publishing, 2000), x.

16. Evelyn Christenson, *What Happens When Women Pray* (Wheaton: Victor, 1975), 142.

17. Christenson, *What God Does,* 88.

Chapter 9: How to Finish Well

1. Kathleen Fischer, *Winter Grace* (New York: Paulist Press, 1985), 1.

2. George Barna, "Family and Personal Accomplishments Lead People's List of Success Determinants," *Barna Research Online,* 6 November 2002, http://www.barna.org/cgi-bin/PagePressRelease. asp?PressReleaseID=124&Reference=A (accessed 11 July 2002).

3. Buford, *Game Plan,* 143.

4. Rick Warren, *The Purpose Driven Life: What on Earth Am I Here For?* (Grand Rapids: Zondervan, 2002), 312.

5. Mikey's Funnies, http://www.youthspecialties.com/free/humor/mikeysfunnies.

6. Willard, *The Divine Conspiracy,* 379.

7. Paul Tournier, *Learn to Grow Old* (New York: Harper & Row, 1972), 119.

8. Willard, *The Divine Conspiracy,* 396. (In his final chapter, "The Restoration of All Things," Willard writes a powerful rationale for the expectations believers have of the continuance of personal awareness in eternity.)

9. Herr, *Lord Show Me Your Glory,* 218. Used by permission of Christian Publications, Inc. 800.233.4443, www.Christianpublications.com

Appendix C

1. Dawson, *Intercession, Thrilling and Fulfilling,* 74–78.

Lorry Lutz is currently a senior associate with Women of Global Action. She has spent a lifetime in foreign mission service both at home and abroad; worked as a magazine editor; and for the last decade served as international coordinator of the AD2000 Women's Track. She is the author of eight other books, including *Women as Risk-Takers for God.* She and her husband, Allen, live in Colorado Springs.